Endorsements

"Lori Rubenstein's newest book, *Forgiveness: Heal Your Past and Find the Peace You Deserve* is a sacred creation, written with love, compassion and of course forgiveness! I found validation that I am on the right path, while giving me the understanding and tools on how to complete my journey to forgiving myself. Lori's gentle spirit and compassion for others shines through in every page. Combining her experience, guidance and expertise with that of other authors, *Forgiveness: Heal Your Past and Find the Peace You Deserve* is just what is needed in the world today! Thank you Lori, for being willing to follow the guidance and write this amazing book!"

~ **Christina Lufkin**,
Author of *Live with Purpose: Die with Dignity*

"Certain writers seem to have the skill to pluck just the right heartstrings at the right time. In her latest book, "*Forgiveness: Heal Your Past and Find the Peace YOU Deserve,*" Lori Rubenstein has not only found her way to my heartstrings, she is playing a symphony. As long as we live in a human skin there will be a necessity for each of us to practice forgiveness. It is not a matter of "if" we need to practice the sacred art of forgiveness – it's a matter of "for whom and when." Quite often that process begins with the one we see staring back at us in the mirror, which then allows us to extend forgiveness to those who occupy our everyday world . . . and beyond. Lori is the perfect messenger for this topic because she practices what she teaches. The question is: Can you use more inner peace in your life? If your answer is yes, then reading this book is not optional – consider it a prerequisite to creating the life you know you really deserve."

~ Dennis Merritt Jones,
Author of *The Art of Uncertainty – How to Live in the Mystery of Life and Love It* and
The Art of Being – 101 Ways to Practice Purpose in Your Life
www.DennisMerrittJones.com

"Forgiveness is a toughie. Some of our biggest life's challenges lie in this conversation. Lori's book provides exquisite guidance while offering you emotional and spiritual insights that are refreshing, practical and healing. Take the ride. I highly recommend it."

~ Shawne Duperon,
6-Time EMMY Winner, Project: Forgive Founder

"There are shelves of books on spiritual transformation and enough self-help publications to keep one busy for several lifetimes. What you don't often find is a successful melding of the two. Lori Rubenstein's newest release, *Forgiveness: Heal Your Past and Find the Peace You Deserve,* is one of the exceptions."

~ Sunny Dawn Johnston,
Author of *Invoking The Archangels – A Nine-Step Process to Healing Your Body, Mind, and Soul*

"How would your life be different if you realized and embraced every challenge as a gift and a blessing? Within these pages are heartfelt stories filled with wisdom, insight, inspiration, forgiveness and love. These men and women have forgiven the unforgivable, and in doing so are now living a life filled with inner peace, balance, understanding and a greater sense of love for ALL. Journey with them from out of the darkness into the light of love, and discover how their lessons can change your life."

~ Sharon Lund, DD,
Author of *The Integrated Being: Techniques to Heal Your Mind-Body-Spirit* and *There Is More . . . 18 Near-Death Experiences*

"Stories of traumatic events are often replayed in the mind again and again. These replays can hold one hostage long after the event has come and gone, making someone a victim of their past. Author of *Forgiveness: Heal Your Past and Find the Peace You Deserve* Lori Rubenstein skillfully shares how to be released from the story and step on the path toward a victorious, empowering life."

~ Sarah McLean,
best-selling Author of *Soul-Centered: Transform Your Life in 8 Weeks with Meditation*

"When I was living life as a victim, all I could see were the obstacles on the path. Lori's book, *Forgiveness: Heal Your Past and Find the Peace YOU Deserve* gives readers a new path to follow, one without guilt or shame, anger or bitterness. If you are ready to forgive yourself or others, this book is the perfect tool."

~ Lori Rekowski,
Author of *A Victim No More* and *Faces Behind the Pages that Inspire*

"Are you eager to live your inspired life but are weighted down by past disappointments? Then you are ready to forgive and Lori Rubenstein's new book, *Forgiveness: Heal Your Past and Find the Peace You Deserve*, is you personal guide to release the wounds of the past and say, "Yes," to your hearts desire."

~ **Susyn Reeve**.
best-selling Author of *The Inspired Life* and the co-founder of www Self-Esteem-Experts.com

"I've known Lori for many years and in every way I've seen she walks the talk. In a world where daily hurts and tribulations are thrusted upon us, it is not always easy to stay centered, walking the talk. True leaders encourage us to move ahead by example. This has been my experience with Lori Rubenstein.

"So is this just another forgiveness book? No! If you are picking up this book, then it is just the message you need. If you're ready to let go of the pain and hurts of your past, and reclaim your power to move forward, then read *Forgiveness: Heal Your Past and Find the Peace You Deserve.* Then when you get the chance, attend or listen to one of Lori's workshops."

~ **Ken Dauth**,
Author of *Beyond the Battlefield: A Message from the Fallen*

"After 35 years as a Psychologist and a Regression Therapist, I have learned, whether examining the happenings in our current life or a past life, that we have all acted or been acted upon in harmful and unhealthy ways. By releasing others, as well as ourselves, from being held captive due to our human behavior choices, we assist ourselves and the planet as a whole, to advance into a peaceful community where everyone is valued. When we Forgive, and let go of the intense emotions of anger, rage, guilt, and shame over what was 'done to us' in the past, it leaves room for our divinity to shine through. Lori Rubenstein's book, *Forgiveness: Heal the Past and Find the Peace YOU Deserve* teaches us how to do that and puts us solidly on the path to create a sense of balance and peace today."

~ Dr. Linda Backman,
Psychologist/Regression Therapist,
Author of *Bringing Your Soul to Light: Healing through Past Lives and the Time Between*
www.RavenHeartCenter.com

"Forgiveness is the most powerful spiritual tool available. Practicing it will empower one to such personal freedom that life becomes an easy flow of experiences that nurture and excite. Lori's book provides a solid and practical foundation for utilizing the power of forgiveness to change your life easily and rapidly. This book is a great gift for yourself and others!"

~ Jamye Price,
Spiritual Teacher, Writer, Channel,
www.crystallinesoulhealing.com

"Lori gets to the heart of the matter when it comes to divorce and dealing with the real issues that count. Life isn't about the "stuff," although in a divorce that is what often takes center stage. Lori's advice and guidance regarding forgiveness and moving on are the real core issues every divorcing person should focus on."

~Dan Couvrette,
CEO - Divorce Marketing Group and Divorce Magazine,
www.DivorceMagazine.com

"Rubenstein calls us all to become our very best selves, and shows us how using forgiveness to get us there. She brings a wonderful blend of wisdom, lightness and vibrancy to every page, while laying out an easy to follow road-map. This book is a treasure for anyone struggling or feeling stuck. If enough people read this book, and do the forgiveness processes, I believe we just may step into that golden age of love and happiness that she talks about!"

~ Eileen Barker, JD,
Author of *The Forgiveness Workbook*

"*Forgiveness: Heal Your Past and Find the Peace You Deserve,* is exactly the step-by-step manual to using forgiveness to heal your life that everyone will benefit from. Forgiveness has played an important role in my healing, and I know it can for you too. There are techniques here for everyone! For me, I particularly love the vision of the peaceful future that can be ours which is painted in this book. I highly recommend this powerful and transformational book to anyone who is ready to the next step in healing."

~ Michele Penn,
Award Winning Photographer and Co-creator of
Peace in the Present Moment (with Eckert Tolle and Byron Katie)
www.creativeelegancebymichele.com

I just wanted you to know how much your Forgiveness Course has helped me coming to terms with the behavior of a close relative of mine. The great thing about this course was that it forced me to ask myself some serious questions why I found it so difficult to forgive that person. Some of the questions are hard but necessary. I was able to admit that I felt I could not forgive until that person had apologized to me. Well – I managed to forgive her even though I know she will probably never apologize, and this realization has brought me peace and emotional calmness anytime I think about her. I highly recommend your book or e-mail course to all who have issues in their lives which trouble them.

~ **Edith Carter**,
Roseburg, Oregon

"Many books have been written about spiritual transformation, many have been written about forgiveness. But nothing has been written on how to achieve a spiritual transformation through forgiveness in such a detailed, empowering way until now. Forgiveness: Heal Your Past and Find the Peace YOU Deserve has provided a roadmap for all who seek to have the life they desire in such a heartfelt way. Rubenstein has given all of us a powerful way to love again!"

~ **Anthony Diaz, JD**,
Inspirational Empowerment Facilitator and Coach,
www.AnthonyJDiaz.com

Forgiveness

Forgiveness:

Heal Your Past and Find the Peace You Deserve

Lori S. Rubenstein

Sacred Life Publishers ™
www.sacredlife.com
United States of America

FORGIVENESS: HEAL YOUR PAST AND FIND THE PEACE YOU DESERVE

FORGIVENESS: HEAL YOUR PAST AND FIND THE PEACE YOU DESERVE can be ordered through booksellers or by contacting:

Lori S. Rubenstein at
www.LoriRubenstein.com

ISBN: 0982233167
ISBN: 978-0-9822331-6-0
Library of Congress Control Number: 2012917742

The information, ideas, and suggestions in this book are not intended as a substitute for professional advice. Before following any suggestions contained in this book, consult your physician or mental health professional. Neither the author nor the publisher shall be liable or responsible for any loss or damage allegedly arising as a consequence of your use or application of any information or suggestions in this book.

Edited by Lori Noble
Cover Design by Lisa Love, www.LisaLove.us

Sacred Life Publishers
www.sacredlife.com
Printed in the United States of America

"The past is over. It doesn't matter who we are, where we came from, what Mommy said, what Daddy did, what mistakes were made, what diseases we have or how depressed we feel. The future can be reprogrammed at this moment."

~ Marianne Williamson

Contents

Section 3
Living with Forgiveness

Introduction

Introduction

> *"We are not held back by the love we didn't receive in the past, but by the love we're not extending in the present."*
>
> *~ Marianne Williamson*

I guess everyone who writes a book hopes it has a profound impact on the readers; I am no exception.

Since there are many "forgiveness" books out there in the world, I had to ask myself, why am I supposed to write another one? I can tell you I believe spirit is working through me and is taking my hand and leading me. In fact, this book feels like a new lover to me. It fills me with love, passion, and excitement. I look forward to writing with "baited breath," counting the hours until we meet again. Every aspect seems to come together, Divine timing, Divine Guidance, Divine Cooperation of the writers, channelers, friends and the publishing. It is like a sacred marriage.

I'm one of those people who other people just feel comfortable enough to "tell me their stories." I can hold the space with grace and non-judgmental love for their healing to take place. I'm told these qualities will come through in this book – hopefully you will agree.

This book is comprised of three sections. Section one expands our knowledge base about what forgiveness is, what it is not and why it is vital in our lives today. Section two gives real life scenarios to help and inspire you to do your own forgiveness work. In this section, each chapter ends with the 4-step Living with Forgiveness Process so you can see how it works. We are asked to practice forgiveness regularly so we build our forgiveness muscle and when the big whammies in life come our way, we can handle them with even more grace. Section three concludes the book with a number of other forgiveness processes and meditations. Play with these and see what works best for you.

In many of the personal stories in this book, you will be introduced to the miracles brought about by forgiveness. It is my belief that in this new golden era of ours, the energies into which we are stepping will allow us all to remember who we are at a core level: spiritual beings having human experiences. When we remember this, our thoughts, values, and actions naturally follow. As we change our perceptions, and rise above holding onto past grudges, hurt, anger and fear, the energies and perceptions of others around us will naturally and miraculously also change.

The 'living with forgiveness' process you will be introduced to supports you in moving through the process of telling your story, acknowledging and accepting the facts of what happened; taking personal responsibility either for what happened or your choice in how to view it; finding the gifts or the lessons in the situation; and then being grateful for those gifts. Being able to stay in gratitude is a huge step towards enlightenment and being the hero of your own story. Living forgiveness is the first step towards living with the understanding there is truly nothing to forgive. Living a life in *oneness* means nothing happens TO us, but rather, FOR us.

As spiritual beings having a human experience, we are here to learn lessons. We are truly a team, working together for our unified soul's growth. Living as ONE means nothing happens to us, but rather, for us.

The quote in the box above is the premise of this book. I understand you might have a different spiritual perspective. There is room in forgiveness for all perspectives. Staying open, nonjudgmental and filling our hearts with acceptance is the key. Our destination is the way back to love, and we will all get there.

Many of us have heard of the ascended master Saint Germain. When I asked my friend Tarri to channel a forgiveness message from him, I should have known it would end up being the introduction to the book! Well, just read and enjoy and you will see what I mean!

Forgiveness Is a Gift You Give Yourself

Saint Germain channeled through
Tarri Otterlee

Let us begin by introducing myself: I AM Saint Germain, an ascended master from The White Brotherhood "The Council of Light." I have lived many physical lifetimes; my last was as the Count of Saint Germain. In that lifetime and other lifetimes, I was an alchemist, healer and spiritual teacher and, like each of you, I continued my learning and personal growth through life lessons and Spirit on my journey Home.

For many hundreds of years it has been taught to forgive those who trespass against us. What does that really mean to you?

Forgiveness of others for the pain they caused you emotionally, physically or economically, whether it was intentional or unintentional, is perhaps the greatest gift of healing you can give yourself. For if you do not do this, or until you are able to forgive, you will be holding anger, bitterness, resentment or hatred in your heart and you cannot move forward to find inner peace, or a more fulfilling life for yourself while holding onto all that no longer serves you. Within this process, you must also forgive yourself for the pain you caused another person intentionally or unintentionally. Whether you want to recognize it or not, you did play a part in creating the bad situation/ relationship or allowed it, perhaps by giving your personal power away (not having healthy boundaries) or just making a bad choices. Of course, there are exceptions to this such as being a victim of rape, robbery, embezzlement etc... but this too, my children, must be forgiven so that you may heal your life and move forward to create happiness where suffering was.

Forgiveness is a great step in healing your heart and soul. The next great step is, never accept bad behavior again and learn healthy boundaries. Without both of these, you will recreate the same negative reality back into your life.

Those negative emotions of bitterness, resentment and getting even with the person you feel did you wrong, only hurts you. The other person usually has moved out of your life and on to the next lesson in their life. These emotional feelings are created by your ego mind and not your heart or soul, for they desire you be at peace and find greater happiness in life. Your life will not feel better and become whole until you heal and forgive others and yourself. This is in itself, a new path to a more fulfilling life with greater inner peace and harmony. Would you rather be right (the ego speaking) or happy (the heart speaking)?

Forgiveness, as a part of your healing journey, is emptying your mind and heart of the negativity that was created there. You must now refill the void or your ego will make sure it will be refilled with more of the same that you have experienced. To refill the void with the positive, you may create a personal prayer and mantra to use daily. We recommend that you also add gratitude to your daily life. There is always something to be grateful for in your day, no matter how bad you think it was. An Attitude of Gratitude creates more blessings and good people to enter your life to be grateful for.

A good life is what you can create in your reality. But, if you remain in anger, bitterness, hatred or revenge, this will continue to manifest over and over again in your life. What you think is what you create consciously or unconsciously. It is simple physics; your thoughts are energy. It is this energy that manifests your life whether it be positive or negative. Forgiveness changes these negative thoughts and energies, allowing the new and the positive thoughts to come into your life to manifest a life filled with inner peace, harmony and love. Gratitude is the way to increase positive thoughts and energies to help you create a new life filled with love and abundance.

Is it time for you to forgive and release people, places and/or things that no longer serve you? Are the choices you make for your highest good, and/or the highest good of others? If not, then perhaps you have more lessons to learn from that person, relationship or situation that you have created in your life now. Or, does your ego love the drama and negativity it produces?

You have chosen this life to experience the physical to learn and grow through your heart and souls evolution. This physical world has much duality and negativity to rise above, so we say to all of you, chose wisely and listen to your heart and your higher consciousness, which is your soul. Your heart and soul does not lead you down the same path that your ego does. Learn to be the master of your ego not the ego as your master.

Use forgiveness of others and self. Set healthy boundaries. Use attitude of gratitude. Your life is now in a positive shift.

This is 2012 The Great Shift of Awakening. It is your shift into a higher consciousness, to create a more abundant life for yourself and for the greater good of all people on planet Earth. Remember you are all from Spirit and will return to Spirit, so we say, "enjoy your journey Home".

Namaste and God bless you all.

Saint Germain in great gratitude to our
Channel Tarri Otterlee
Sedona, Arizona

There is a piece of me that feels so honored to be chosen to be here today to help usher in this new energy. I feel a sense of responsibility to teach whatever I know to others. I am also like a sponge, soaking up the information coming my way from other sources. Living in the Sedona area, I am in the heart of spiritual energies and resources and I am fortunate to have the support of some of those resources in this book. You will be introduced to six channels from enlightened masters and spiritual beings, and you will read personal, heartfelt stories of forgiveness and transformation from those who have experienced it first hand. I hope you resonate with them and allow them to guide you to take the next step in your evolutionary path . . . on the way back to love.

May the natural progression of forgiveness flow in and out, weaving its healing power all throughout your life.

Section 1:

Finding and Opening the Door to Forgiveness

Chapter 1

Creating a New Golden Age

The Path to Personal and World Peace Starts with Forgiveness

Forgiveness is probably the most divine act we can do. It's one of those things we count on God to do for us. What if we follow the lead of the God within?

We've all heard it: In 2012, the Mayan calendar ends, the earth is shifting, massive economic collapse, the Arab spring, and of course, apocalyptic/end of the world predictions. What you might not have heard is that many indigenous cultures see this time in history as the end of one cycle and the beginning of a new one. We, as a society, are at a *choice point.*[1] We can create a golden age or bring in an age of continued darkness and destruction. I desire the vision of a new golden age. What about you?

The veil between human/earth life and what we call "life after death" or the "hereafter" is thinning. People having "near death experiences" come back and report we are all connected, we must learn to love, and we must stop thinking we are all separate from one another. Others, through past life and in-between life regressions, report not only past lives on earth and other planets, but also of being able to see where they go as Spirit in-between those lifetimes. Even more proof of the thinning of the veil is that numerous people are having conversations with people who have passed over. Many report feeling and seeing non-human energies, hearing them, and smelling them. Other people are channeling masters, guides and angels. It is now commonly accepted by millions that **we are spiritual beings having a human experience**. We come to the earth to learn lessons which are best learned in a place of duality. Some of these lessons are learning to trust ourselves, creating boundaries, learning how to communicate, and learning how to live in integrity. [2]

An example of why we chose to live in duality is this: If you came to learn how to create boundaries, you might have to experience abuse and teach yourself how to assert clear boundaries. In experiencing the lack of boundaries, you have to learn that you are in fact worth sticking up for.

In other words, every time we "overcome a hardship" or "find our self-value" we incorporate another lesson into our spirit. Our vibration rises and we move forward on our path back to love/God/Universal Oneness. And as each individual does their own work, and expands their own vibration, it spreads out and resonates with others. One by one, we make a difference.

With these concepts in mind, time is of the essence. If there is a chance that we who have chosen to be on the earth in this era of transformation are responsible for the direction we take as a human race, then we might want to get serious about our growth. If it is true that what we think, what we create, and the choices or decisions we make have huge cones-quences for the human race, we must call forth our inner strength and act from a place of integrity and responsibility – not someday, right now! Why take chances? It is imperative to wake up, step up, and be the very best human ambassadors we can be. We can not reach enlightenment without acceptance and learning to release judgment. If a golden age of peace is to come, we need to first stop our inner wars, stop our destructive self-loathing, and learn how to accept, release, forgive, and love ourselves and others. This is the intention of this book. This book is a guide towards learning to accept, release, forgive, and love as we learn to stop the inner wars and destructive self-loathing.

If a golden age of peace is to come, we need to first stop our inner wars, stop our destructive self-loathing, and learn how to accept, release, forgive, and love ourselves and others.

This book teaches us that one of the ways we find our way back to love is through the miracle of the gift of forgiveness. By this I mean we need to get back to living from our soul's intention, rather than living from ego or fear. What I have learned over the years is when you remove the layers of hurt, fear, anger, frustration, bitterness, confusion, neediness, shame and guilt, what you have left is a beautiful, multi-faceted diamond of love, with all its facets shining brightly. Moreover, when you are living from the place of clarity, love, compassion, acceptance, and non-judgment, the universe conspires to meet your needs and desires and you are content with whatever shows up in your life. Once you choose to change your perspective, everything life offers you is meaningful and filled with grace.

What does grace look like? Grace is a divine and sacred gift from God and is available to everyone. It allows us to release and let go. It's a gift of mercy, giving us peace. What does this look like in everyday life? It's simple; I found it recently when I ran into an old acquaintance, a lovely spiritual-based woman in the grocery store! She told me she just lost her job and was wrongfully accused of something. It took some time, but she forgave her accusers and realized how peaceful her life has been since she lost the job. The fact is, she had wanted to quit for some time anyway, but 'could not afford to do so.' She now sees the blessing in the firing, and is grateful for the outcome. I know you understand exactly what I am saying here.

There are many lenses through which we see, and we all have the choice of which lens to see through. Certainly it hurts to be fired, especially for something you did not do. You can choose the lens of anger, the lens of retaliation, or the lens of the martyr, and no one will blame you. All of those lenses make sense, but none of them will lead to a happy, soul-centered life. Recognizing the grace in all things, the gift of getting what she wanted even though the way it happened is not of her design, takes practice. It takes building your forgiveness muscle to see clearly and accept with grace.

Building your forgiveness muscle is about training and practice. In the very same week, I got to see first hand with another friend what training and practicing forgiveness looks like. My friend told me she and her boyfriend were fighting. She went for a walk to take some time before responding to him. During the walk, she realized she could go back and fight it out to prove her point, but she knew what she really wanted to do was to forgive and let it go. She understood in the bigger scheme of things, this argument was unimportant, a thing of the past. So she CHOSE to forgive and live from the place of "this too shall pass!" She felt peaceful, blissful actually, choosing to live in the energy of what she called ACCEPTANCE. She went back home and was able to let go of "being right." And, she was able to forgive not only him for "hurting her feelings" but herself for blaming, judging, and projecting her pain upon him. It's natural to want retribution and it's easy to blame others, which is why practicing forgiveness on a regular basis allows us to release karma, guilt, and shame. When whole communities start treating each other, and themselves, in this way, we see miracles. Our collective stories will change. With oneness, we allow space for this new golden era to enter.

> *"The truth of who you are is in between the dreams of who you think you are. Walk lightly and be the observer of the dream. You are neither of them, but the one who dreams. In truth, you are me and I am you."*
>
> *~ Lori Noble*

In this new era, we wake up from the conscious dream of duality, knowing that we can only see as far as Earth's duality can take us. We make the choice to leave the drama-trauma behind and choose to see things from a more sacred and higher vantage point. The bottom line is that what we see from the world of duality, from right/wrong or left versus right brain thinking is very limited. The 'Living with Forgiveness' process taught in this book will help us change how we think and will open us up to possibilities that at this point, are beyond our imagination.

~~~***~~~
~~~

Chapter 2

A Course in Courage

Lessons that Teach Us Why Forgiveness Is So Necessary in Our Lives

> *"Life is too short for drama and petty things, so kiss slowly, laugh insanely, love truly and forgive quickly."*
>
> *~ Author Unknown*

We need forgiveness in our lives if we experience hurt, anger, bitterness, or resentment. Forgiveness allows us to be happy and to feel peace. It gives us freedom and it is good for our health. Even guilt and self-loathing fall away in the face of forgiveness.

The stories we tell ourselves when we come from the place of being hurt, injured, or resentful are very different from the stories we tell ourselves when we have been transformed. Throughout this book, you will find many examples of how forgiveness transforms people's lives. You will see how their "stories" have changed as a result of their own forgiveness. Self esteem is magnified when we go through a forgiveness process, because we know we can be injured, and then we can recover. We learn who we are in truth, cannot really be injured.

> *"There is no single effort more radical in its potential for saving the world than a transformation of the way we raise our children."*
>
> ~ Marianne Williamson

Children learn what they are taught

Let us take a common example. Imagine two children, Johnny and Jimmy, are teased at school. Both children are called "stupid" by a little boy in their class, and they both go home and tell their parents. Their parents' reactions can have lifetime ramifications with regard to each of the boy's self-esteem and self-confidence.

Johnny's mother is outraged, takes her child by the hand, goes to the school, and demands retribution. The offending child must be punished! Look at poor Johnny, helpless, injured, and victimized. Johnny is taught 'eye for an eye, tooth for a tooth' justice and he learns in order to feel better about an incident, the offender must be punished. Otherwise, there is no justice, and the injury remains. Johnny does not learn self-care. Instead, Johnny learns victimization.

Jimmy's mother asks him if what the bully said is true and asks, "If it is not true, why would it bother you?" A conversation then ensues about why people choose to hurt others with their words. Jimmy's mother might say, "If it still bothers you, you have some choices. 1. Do not play with that child anymore. 2. Create a boundary by telling the child he hurt your feelings and you don't want him to treat you like this anymore. 3. Forgive the child for he obviously doesn't understand how hurtful words are, or he is hearing mean things being said at home. 4. Pray for the child, and send the child love, because the child needs some extra love." Jimmy's mother might even help Jimmy choose what FEELS right for him. Which option gives him the most energy? She might teach Jimmy about weighing choices – looking at the pros and cons of each option. In this scenario, Jimmy definitely learns how to listen to his gut feelings and how to make decisions that work for him. Jimmy learns he is responsible for how he feels and how he responds to someone doing something hurtful to him. This is empowerment, not victimization. These options create self-esteem and self-confidence. Forgiveness flows easily because Jimmy isn't looking at the offender to right the wrong and he learns how he feels about himself is up to him, not other people. Wow! I wish I understood this when my children were young!

Our children need to be taught how to think, not what to think.

So it is easy to see, from the point of view of a child, why forgiveness is necessary from a young age. I propose we all be childlike in our approach to forgiveness. Let us learn from the example above and see the difference forgiveness can make in our lives. If you have been acting like Johnny, looking for retaliation before you can forgive, then pretend to be Jimmy's mother, the one who teaches us to take responsibility for how we feel.

Why is Forgiveness Necessary?

It creates a sense of personal power, self-confidence, and self-esteem. It gives us the ability to know we can get over hurts and injury, whether caused by others or ourselves. Author and Medical Intuitive Carolyn

Myss, in her book, *Entering the Castle: Finding the Inner Path to God and Your Soul's Purpose,* (Free Press, 2008) gives a great example of holding onto hurt. She says it is like being locked in a dungeon, chained to the person who hurt you, for a lifetime. If you think about being chained to the person who injured you, then you might seriously choose to free yourself from those shackles by forgiving the offender.

To GIVE forgiveness to someone else is an amazing gift. So many people walk around feeling guilt and shame and they do not know how to release it. Your generosity in letting someone off the hook teaches them they can do the same, for themselves and others. You are basically teaching them that the guilt they were tightly holding was unnecessary. Can you see how forgiving is one of those 'pay it forward' kinds of concepts? It is intergenerational, and it creates a whole new paradigm in our families, communities, and eventually, the world. This is not Pollyanna thinking. This is a one-step, one-person-at-a-time transformation.

To GIVE forgiveness to YOURSELF is the best gift of all! It is precious and has long lasting ramifications. First of all, if you are a person who lives with guilt, you will likely try to manipulate others with guilt. Second, if you live as an injured, hurt person, then you will continue to attract injured, hurt people into your life. You can't create a healthy relationship with others when you yourself are not healthy. Third, if you do not forgive yourself, then you are likely to cause yourself physical harm from all the stress and guilt you carry. See chapter 4 on Forgiveness and Health.

Have you ever had someone not forgive you even though you've asked for forgiveness?[3] Can you imagine your entire life being based on something hurtful you did to someone else 30 years ago? Yet, for many people, this is reality. They carry self-blame, guilt, and shame throughout their lifetimes. And some choose to spend their entire lifetime blaming someone else for their hurts and anger.

Please take some time and start thinking and start writing:

Who do you need to forgive?

What hurt, anger, resentment or bitterness is still residing in you?

Who have you hurt in your past?

What guilt are you holding onto?

How are you keeping others chained in the dungeon, who can you release?

What Forgiveness is NOT:

I cannot tell you how important it is to understand what forgiveness is not. This is the 'meat and potatoes' of forgiveness. For you vegetarians, this is the 'tofu veggie green curry' special. I believe with all my heart and soul that false beliefs about what forgiveness is keeps people from forgiving. I bear witness to this over and over again with myself and my clients.

For many years, I knew I needed to forgive my father, but I was stuck in being "right" and believed what he did was "wrong." If you are shaking your head yes right now, you know exactly what I am talking about. I thought, "OK, if he asks for forgiveness, since he's my father, I will give it to him, but he needs to be really sorry first!" As a consequence of this right/wrong thinking I was chained to bitterness and resentment towards my father for years.

When my ex-husband hurt me deeply in our marriage, I really struggled over deciding whether I would choose to forgive him. As an attorney, I continued to live in the right/wrong model of the world. So, I could argue and prove his wrongness. His "wrongness" made me a victim, and as a victim, I was powerless to forgive. I also thought at the time, if I forgave him it would let him off the hook. I certainly could not allow myself to let go of the notion that he should feel guilty forever! I thought by forgiving him I needed to get back together and trust him again. In fact, I did try to get back together and the trust was broken three times before I realized "This isn't working!" I also thought to forgive him was the equivalent of endorsing his bad behavior. Well, there was no way my inflexible thinking would allow for such a thing! Can you see where he was in the dungeon and I was chained to him by my inability to forgive? With this much anger, hurt, bitterness, rejection, and feelings of abandonment, I was a train-wreck of a victim!

So, the bottom line, what really blocked me from forgiveness, from finding peace in my inner life, was my misconceptions about forgiveness. I had to first learn what forgiveness is NOT before I could choose to do it.

I learned that forgiving

1. **is not about me being stupid or being a fool;**
2. **is not about forgetting what happened;**
3. **is not a sign of weakness or neediness;**
4. **does not mean I must trust him again;**
5. **does not mean I am letting him off the hook;**
6. **does not mean I must reunite with him;**
7. **does not mean what he did was OK or I must endorse his bad behavior;**
8. **is not about him being good or bad;**
9. **is not about whether he is sorry and feels adequately ashamed and bad for what he did;**
10. **is not about my duty to punish someone for their behavior as though I was the Karma Guard, God, Judge, Jury and Prosecutor all at once;**
11. **does not mean I had to even the score and "show him"; and**
12. **does not mean I instantly feel at peace.**

You can see there are many reasons people resist forgiveness. Years ago I would watch Oprah interview people who forgave their rapist or the person who murdered their beloved family member. I would think "How could they forgive and let this person off the hook?" I almost felt it was my duty to stay mad at the person for them! They were slackers, weak, for not maintaining their anger at their offender!

I was shocked to learn it was the other way around. In my experience, forgiveness has been a kind of freedom and grace which I receive once I make the decision to let go of the pain another has caused me. I am not asked to give away what I don't have, but to receive what I need.

We are reminded by Mahatma Gandhi, "If we practice an eye for an eye and tooth for a tooth, soon the whole world will be blind and toothless." Is this what we really want?

Without forgiveness, we are trapped. We are trapped in our pain, chained to the person who hurt us, and blocked from all we desire in life. Forgiveness frees us and puts us back on the path of love, freedom, happiness and hope.

What has gotten in the way of you forgiving? What misconceptions have you held onto about forgiveness?

What if the belief you held onto about forgiveness simply is not true?

Are you ready to look at the truth of forgiveness?

What Forgiveness IS:

Forgiving is pure, unadulterated, self-centered self-interest and self-care. We don't choose to forgive because it helps someone else. We choose forgiveness because it helps US. This ultimately means forgiveness has nothing to do with the other person. This is about YOU – YOUR health, YOUR happiness, YOUR freedom from pain and YOUR personal and spiritual growth.

Tony Robbins says happiness is based in large part upon how flexible you are. In other words, people who see the world in a black and white manner are less happy than those who can see and accept the various shades of grey. Forgiveness helps us get out of black and white thinking by releasing the attachment to right/wrong and victim/offender mentality.

From a more spiritual perspective, I have learned no one else hurts you. When another person acts, you personally choose how you want to respond or how you want to feel about the particular incident. (We see this clearly with the example of the two school-aged children at the beginning of this chapter.) Of course, it doesn't always seem so conscious. It may just be how we have programmed ourselves to react. It feels automatic and it may feel like the stimulus created the feeling. However, it truly is your choice and is within your control to change how you respond.

Forgiveness has nothing to do with the other person . . .
it has everything to do with you!

Choosing how you want to respond and how you feel is totally up to you!

Once we are free of our misconceptions, we can begin to learn what forgiveness is.

Forgiveness is about

1. **taking responsibility for your own actions and feelings;**
2. **taking responsibility for not letting the hurt you suffered continue to eat at you;**
3. **getting out of the victim role and taking back, or creating, control over your life;**
4. **ensuring your survival and welfare;**
5. **learning to trust your own instincts and taking care of yourself;**
6. **learning how to stand up for your needs by speaking your truth and creating boundaries as necessary;**
7. **getting in touch with a more flexible way of thinking and seeing the world as flexible;**

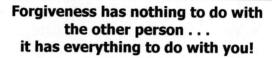

8. **allowing for grace and miracles to become a part of your life;**
9. **living a healthier lifestyle, and being mindful of your thoughts and reactions;**
10. **learning to see the gift in every situation;**
11. **finding self-acceptance and judging others (and yourself) less; and**
12. **finding true happiness and peace within yourself.**

Forgiveness comes from a place of strength, courage, resolve and responsibility. And like a muscle, the more you use it, the stronger it becomes.

Remember the story when Jeshua asked for the person without sin to cast the first stone? Well, every one of us has hurt someone with our actions or words at some point in our life. How would it feel if you were never forgiven? How would you feel if something you did 20 years ago was still used against you? How would you feel if **you** were still judged by that past incident?

If you have a choice between carrying a very heavy load up hill and using a cart to wheel the load, you would use the cart, right? Well, it is the same with the anger, fear and disappointment that comes from hurt. Think of forgiveness as your cart. Rather than carrying the weight of it all alone, you can put it in the cart (you still know it is there, you have not forgotten about it) but it is no longer attached to you. Your body, heart and soul will no longer be injured by the extra load (the hurt you feel by not forgiving) you carry.

How do we Forgive?

Forgiveness is a multi-level approach toward freeing yourself from the past. As is said in alcohol treatment, you talk the talk, walk the walk and finally feel the feelings. I felt guilty and frustrated for years because I could not "feel" forgiveness. I thought I was a "forgiveness fake" for a long time. Even years later, after I decided to forgive, I still felt hurt and disappointed. I thought, "What is wrong with me? Why am I not able to really forgive?"

I was stuck in another forgiveness fallacy. I thought if I didn't feel better once I decided to forgive, I must have done it wrong. I had to learn forgiveness follows its own time schedule. I can't control it. Forgiving is kind of like planting a seed. You make the decision to plant it. You nurture the soil and take the steps to allow it to grow. But you don't get to decide when it flowers. You just trust the process, and know that one day you will turn around and find forgiveness flourishing in your life as if it was always there.

This series of exercises will help you prepare to work through the process of forgiveness. Trust them, trust yourself, and trust the healing power of forgiveness. **While you go through them, remember that it is OK at first to just be talking the talk.** Saying and thinking "I forgive" is enough. Eventually, as you do more of the exercises throughout this book you will begin walking the walk and by the time you complete the 'Living with Forgiveness' exercises, you will feel, know, and "be" forgiveness. Also, remember YOU ARE

NOT DOING THIS ALONE. You have the spiritual strength of your higher self (who is an expert on forgiveness) to guide you.

Letting Go

When you feel hurt and angry, it's hard to think about forgiving. We often get stuck in the space of "being right" and the other person "being wrong." We certainly get frustrated when our expectations are not met. When we look below the surface, we know our hurt and anger is hurting ourselves, but honestly, it is easier to blame someone else. My friend Barry calls this a "miss-expression." Since we only control ourselves and our own thoughts, we must accept responsibility for the thoughts we think about the incident. Knowing how we want to respond and how we want to express ourselves is important.

Let's face it: Most of us are not Mother Teresa, nor are we those people we see on Oprah who forgive their rapist or father's murderer so easily. Most of us intellectually understand the truth – we are hurting ourselves by hanging onto the anger and reliving the pain every time our angry heart thinks about the situation. We may even understand that we are allowing someone else's actions to control us today. So we have to make a choice – the choice NOT to let our thoughts destroy us, the choice to let go of those limiting thoughts. Just let them go.

When are we really being foolish? When we allow the pain of the past to hurt us and control us in the present.

With the proper tools, we do not have to feel foolish. We do have to be honest with ourselves and ask, "What negative thoughts are going on in my head?" Am I making up a "story" about this situation which is limiting me? If I am going to make something up anyway, why not make up something that serves me, the other person, and the world in a better way? How can I bring the gift of forgiveness to this situation? How can I show compassion in this situation?

We have to learn how to do things differently. You know the old saying – insanity is doing the same thing over and over again and expecting a different result? Well, that's what happens when you refuse to let go.

If the thoughts are too intense and involved, and you feel like you can't stop yourself from negative obsessing. One tool I recommend is tapping, also known as the Emotional Freedom Technique (EFT). For more information, please go to chapter 10 and you will find out more information about EFT and how it can work for you. Another tool my friend Debbie recommends is Ho'oponopono, a simple but compassionate Hawaiian release technique where you say, "I love you, I am sorry, Please forgive me, Thank you!" Now you can do this to yourself if you are mad at yourself, and here is the really cool part. It feels like a paradox, sort of nonsensical when someone hurts you but you are asking them for forgiveness. Yet, it powerfully expresses the spiritual principle: we are all One and when One is forgiven, we are All forgiven.

Changing Perspective

Another helpful tool is to change the way we see things. In other words, *change our perspective.* Let go of the RULES we create about what is right and what is wrong, and about what is acceptable and what is not. This is all about flexibility, and the more flexible we are, the happier our lives are. In truth, all events are neutral. It is just our thoughts or judgments about them that make them different than what they are in truth.

Most of the time, if you are feeling hurt or angry, you have taken on the very unattractive quality of the VICTIM. Do you want to be a victim or act like a victim? Of course not! I can tell you that at the end of my first marriage, I loved playing the victim and casting him in the role of the perpetrator. I was right and he was wrong. I was comfortable with this perspective because it matched a value, a rule, I carried throughout my life that cheating was wrong. And guess what? EVERYONE I knew supported me in this belief. True? I bet you, the reader, might also support me in the belief that cheating is wrong and the person cheated upon is the victim.

The belief that went along with the cheating was he didn't love me. I now understand that this particular belief triggered in me the core internal belief that I was not good enough, I was unlovable! So, if the internal belief is 'I am not good enough' or 'I am unlovable,' and this thought is being sent out into the Universe, and my spouse, the person in my life who I have charged with showing me love, was picking up on this vibration, which came first? What if I knew at that time that I was lovable, loving and loved?

How would choosing this belief have changed the situation?

To change a perspective, we need to be *willing to see* other perspectives, *choose* to see other perspectives, *release* all judgments about the situation, *let go* of the perspective that hurts us, and then *decide* to choose a better, healthier perspective.

Changing perspectives shatters our previous limiting beliefs. I once believed people's actions were either right or wrong and that made *them* right or wrong. Today, I believe we are all pure souls and we have chosen these experiences to further the growth of our souls and our loved ones. And when we are able to choose this higher, healthier perspective, we are well on our way to the prize: Forgiveness of Self.

Now you have clarity about what forgiveness is, what it is not, and why it is so vital to forgive. You've learned a few techniques to help you let go and change your perspective. It's all about flexibility and giving up black and white thinking.

Yes, you've been hurt in the past. However, the truth is something happened and you chose how to perceive the incident. There are numerous ways to respond to any particular event. The decision on how to respond is 100% within your ability to choose.

Here is another way, a new perspective, of how to look at problems, emotional or hurtful events in your life, by Tony Robbins:

Truth about Problems

"Your problem is that you think your problem is the problem.

The real problem is that you think you're not supposed to have problems.

Problems are gifts. Problems stimulate us to grow and give.

The real problem is that you haven't found and embraced an empowering meaning.

If you don't master your perception of things, you cannot master life.

We think we can get rid of problems, but we can't. We can just get better quality problems.

Problems and happiness have no relationship."

~~~***~~~
~~~

Chapter 3

Forgiveness

The Key to Spiritual Enlightenment

> *"People are often unreasonable, illogical, and self-centered. Forgive them anyway.*
>
> *If you are kind, people may accuse you of selfish, ulterior motives.* Be kind anyway.
>
> *If you are successful, you will win some false friends and some true enemies.* Succeed anyway.
>
> *If you are honest and frank, people may cheat you.* Be honest and frank anyway.
>
> *What you spend years building, someone could destroy overnight.* Build anyway.
>
> *If you find serenity and happiness, they may be jealous.* Be happy anyway.
>
> *The good you do today, people will often forget tomorrow.* Do good anyway.
>
> *Give the best you have, and it may never be enough.* Give the best you have anyway.
>
> *You see, in the final analysis, it is between you and God. It was never between you and them anyway."*
>
> ~ Mother Teresa

Our human experiences on earth are created to nourish our soul's growth. We, as souls, chose earth as a good place to learn the lessons we need to learn.

We can embrace those lessons, or we can resist and fight. I am assuming if you've made it this far in the book, you desire to embrace, learn, and grow.[4]

Many masters, gurus, religious leaders, philosophers, spiritual teachers and healers teach us that certain values are embraced by those close to ascension or enlightenment. Among those values are Compassion, Acceptance, Non-judgment, Joy, and Understanding. How do you get to live those values? Through Forgiveness[5] we begin to remove the barriers of the Earthly ego (believing we are separate from God and Spirit) and recognize who we really are, as spiritual beings. Forgiveness helps us step into alignment with these values by releasing judgment, and by learning how to simply 'let go' on a regular basis. I think you would agree that it is hard to think of a compassionate, non-judgmental person who also exudes bitterness, anger or hatred.

> *"There's no reason to feel guilt or shame. No one actually has an ego, they have a thought that they're separate from God and others and that thought started from a metaphor that was misinterpreted and then taught over and over again so that it seemed to be part of the human condition and experience."*
>
> Barbara Lauman,
> *Conversations with my Daughter on the Other Side* (Balboa Press 2012)

As we make our way towards spiritual enlightenment, it is necessary for us to understand on a deeper level the importance of forgiveness for humans and for their souls, I would like to present you with a Channeling from the Light Beings, channeled by Dr. Earl Backman in April 2012.

Forgiveness is a Choice and All Beings are Able to Forgive

LORI: So my question is: Why is forgiveness necessary to further our human and soul's growth, and do you have any recommendations on how to forgive?

> *EARL: Where we like to begin with this and this is where we would have begun if you hadn't asked this question, is to understand the impact of lack of forgiveness on the soul, on the psyche, on the personality. This is important. It is a way of reversing initially what you're looking at and that is forgiveness. So if you look at what happens when one is incapable – chooses not to – refuses – to forgive, forgive themselves or to forgive others. The impact of that is pure unadulterated paralysis because what happens when one does not forgive, is that one chooses then to live in disharmony with one's soul-self. Because one's soul-self is about love, hope, compassion, acceptance, and understanding. These embody the nature of forgiveness. And if you don't relate to yourself from that perspective or to someone else in that perspective, then you are projecting onto them negative feelings that you have. When you contain within your body, these negative feelings, fear and anger, as a result of your refusal to forgive someone else for what they*

did, or yourself for what you have done, then you cut yourself off from your guides and teachers who want to assist you on your soul purpose path. So you lose the ability to connect with those on the other side who are most forgiving.

You must remember that all earth beings have had past lives where they have done things to others, as well as had things done to them that complicated their lives and had a negative impact. Frequently, one brings the karma from a past life and one's inability to forgive others and themselves in a past life, into this life. And they frequently have the opportunity to exercise forgiveness for what occurred in a past life, as well as what has occurred in this life. For often in this particular lifetime, one is meant to delete past life karma with forgiveness. The act of forgiving is the act of releasing. Releasing negativity.

When one holds on to the pain that they feel because of what others may have done to them, when they choose to embrace and hold onto that pain it is a destructive force, there is no net positive gain in holding onto pain. But in order to forgive someone else for their behaviors, you must be willing to forgive yourself. It is like love. You cannot love someone else until you learn to love yourself, so it begins with self. And when we say, begins with self, we're not talking about it begins with ego, we're talking about it begins with self, soul-self.

The act of forgiving is absolutely necessary in order to move forward, to achieve your soul intention in this lifetime. You cannot move forward if you're holding onto pain, anger. The inability to forgive either others or yourself for actions is common. This is an incredibly important subject to understand. For the act of forgiveness is a choice, in that earth beings make the decision to either forgive or not to forgive. When someone says to someone, I cannot forgive you for what you have done or what you have said or the pain you have inflicted on me or whatever. When they say, I cannot forgive you, or if they say, I cannot forgive myself for the pain I have caused you, what they're truly saying is they are ***choosing*** *not to forgive.* ***It is a choice. The "I cannot" is really "I WILL not." Earth beings can forgive, if they choose****. It is really, I will not forgive or I will not forgive you or I will not forgive myself –* ***it is a choice****.*

This is something you need to explore, because many think it is not a choice issue. That they truly have no choice, that is wrong. All earth beings have a choice. You have a choice on how to behave. You have a choice in what to say. And you have a choice to forgive others. And when you, yourself, when you do not forgive others, for pain that you feel has been inflicted on you, then the one holding onto the pain suffers greatly. It is in sense a double suffering. One may feel the pain of what was caused and then the inability to feel forgiveness causes more pain. On the other hand, the one who has caused, or the one who's behavior has inflicted pain, if they forgive from a heartfelt space not from a head space – remember the act of forgiving is not just a left brain action or behavior. The act of forgiving, is like the act of deleting pain or karma. It is a total part of ones body, heart, mind, and soul. If one forgives from both the left brain and the right brain. But it's the right brain where the emotion is attached to it.

But remember, the act of forgiveness, the act of being willing to forgive someone else for behavior that you find inappropriate and in some ways down right abhorrent, that act of forgiving elevates your soul evolution. When you can forgive in the most dire and painful situations, and you know there are many stories of that, stories of loss. Loss caused by the behavior of another person's inattention, and the one's family members who are feeling that loss of a loved one, can forgive that person. The act of forgiveness is an energetic surrounding of love, hope, compassion, acceptance, and understanding. And it spreads outward. When enlightened earth beings hear stories, where individuals genuinely, heartfelt, soul level, forgive someone else for a wide variety of behaviors, it is contagious. Everyone can feel better.

It is so important for us, more than any other concept in this book, to recognize forgiveness is a choice! The stories that follow in Section 2 illustrate perfectly what it is like to move from pain, anger, hurt and confusion through forgiveness to being in a place of peace and freedom.

Forgiveness begins when we come to earth with the concept of forgetting who we are when we are born, feeling separated from God (not recognizing we are in fact God), seeing ourselves through the eyes of our parents and 'others', and going through a process of finding our true self again. We then realize we are all one and there is ultimately nothing to forgive because we are united in our goal of self-growth and the return to love.

I'd like to give you an example of our interconnectedness. I was working with a group of 8th

grade girls and we were talking about the destructiveness of gossip. I wanted to show them energetically how our thoughts have vibrations that affect the person we think about, as well as negatively affecting ourselves when we have those thoughts. We used kinesiology [6] (muscle testing) to do this. Girl A would think bad thoughts about girl B. Girl B would not know if positive or negative thoughts were being directed towards her. She would lift her arm and be asked to hold it strong. Her arm would be weak when the thoughts were negative, and would hold firm when positive. Likewise, when girl A was muscle tested, her body would be weak just from thinking negative thoughts towards girl B.

When we believe we are separate, we can create painful incidents which give us the opportunity we need to explore feelings of hurt, anger and resentment and to over come them. Forgiveness of ourselves, God, and others allows us to clear and release these negative feelings.

As we mature, we make up stories to confirm our experiences. We need to some how make sense of our lives and we do this through the stories we tell ourselves. As children, we were self-centered creatures, so it naturally follows that our stories are all about us. For example, a child who is abused by a parent might create a story of "I'm bad," or "There is something wrong with me."

As we tell ourselves these stories over and over again, they ultimately morph into our core beliefs. As adults we allow these core beliefs to define us. Few of us take the time to ask "Is this true? Where did this belief come from?" And interestingly, the stories we tell ourselves can be empowering stories, or disempowering ones. I want to share with you some simple examples from my own childhood to help you identify your own 'negative' or shadow beliefs. Try to remember what it felt like. Be easy on yourself. Remember, this is a process.

1. Fact as I saw it: My mother was too busy.

Belief I took from it: I wasn't worth her time.

Adult view of the truth: She was just being a teenager.

2. Fact as I saw it: My father left me.

Belief I took from it: He doesn't love me.
I am unlovable.
I am not good enough.

Adult view of the truth: He divorced my mother and saw me weekly.

By the age of 6, I believed my mother would never have time for me, anything I wanted I had to get myself, I was unlovable, I was not good enough, I caused arguments, my parents hated each other and me, and that my needs were not important. When my stepfather also left when I was 12 years of age, I added the belief, "Every man will leave me."

Can you see where I'm going with this? It only makes sense with a story like this that I would try to escape my "reality." So, as a teenager I tried to cover up my emotions through the use of drugs, and I was looking for love in all the wrong places.

It was the act of forgiving or "giving up one story for another" that helped me. On the way to forgiveness, I learned to stop blaming others for my life and began to take personal responsibility for my own life.

Fortunately for me, at age 16, my mother had a wake up call and sent me to a drug rehabilitation center in my sophomore year of high school. I learned my life was the result of **my** choices, and it was my choice how I viewed my life! I could choose to continue those debilitating beliefs, or choose more empowering ones, like "I am smart," "I am competent," and "with my determination and motivation I can do anything I want!" I learned it was within my power to *"change my story."* This was transformative for me. Had I continued the unhealthy thought patterns of "I'm not good enough" and the patterns of blaming others for how my life turned out, the addictive behaviors would have continued and I would not be here today writing this book.

Thought by thought,
you can change
your life for the better.

Learning to take personal responsibility for my actions led me closer to the more enlightened beliefs and values I spoke of earlier: understanding, compassion, self-acceptance and non-judgment. I now realize that my childhood was blessed with gifts, little nuggets of learning and much love. Let us look again at my list of beliefs and how I was able to see, through the grace of choice to change my thoughts and beliefs, the gifts of each situation.

1. My mother didn't have time for me. So, I don't deserve her, or anyone else's, time:

    Gift #1: I learned how to take care of myself.

    Gift #2: I am not needy or dependent.

    Gift #3: I learned to solve my own problems.

2. My father left me. So, I'm unlovable, I'm not good enough. All men will leave me.

    Gift #1: I learned to work and was a full time mother's helper during the summer at age 11.

    Gift #2: I didn't depend on my parents to tell me what I needed or to get it for me. I learned to think independently and get my own needs met.

    Gift #3: I became a little fighter and advocate for the underdog, as I was one too.

    Gift #4: Eventually I even learned to love myself. It took years to forgive my father completely, but when I finally did, I was empowered to step out of the role of victim and then I could really love and respect myself.

Basically, I learned to look through the eyes of forgiveness and develop a clearer perception of life. I realized all those debilitating beliefs were based on **stories** that I made up. As children in a family, we are rarely taught that we are spiritual beings having a human experience, and our thoughts and beliefs are as valid as any one else's, or that our parents are only doing the best they know how to do.

At some point in our respective journeys, we wake up and realize that how we choose to view our lives is a GIFT. In fact, it is the third step in the "living with forgiveness" process. This is the time we release our negative beliefs and find freedom and peace in the release. It is empowering to know our negative beliefs no longer control us, and we can stop judging and blaming our parents for not being who we want them to be. We can then be thankful for the gifts, the lessons, and the personal growth.

By overcoming our negative beliefs, we become our own heroes!

We love the hero's tale, where someone has a rough life, and overcomes all sorts of trials and tribulations. She develops moral strength and character by facing those fears and tribulations. She overcomes something very personal, she shares what she learned, and, in the end, she becomes an inspiration and source of strength to others. You too can be the hero in your own life.

It is time to examine your belief system. Do as I have done above: take a negative belief you have had about yourself from childhood and trace it back to the source of the belief. What was your perspective from childhood? Now, looking at the same belief, how do you see that as an adult?

<u>Fact as YOU saw it:</u>

<u>Belief YOU took from it:</u>

<u>Adult View of the truth:</u>

Now, look at the gifts. How have you benefited from exposure to those incidences? What about your life today is benefiting from that lesson? Take out your journal and write out all the gifts and lessons.

It's interesting; isn't it? In every story, there is a gift. If you can't find the gift to your human/ego self, then look at the gift to your soul. What have you learned? What have you mastered? For example, if you grew up in an alcoholic and abusive household, you might be a great mediator, or be very self-sufficient. There is always a gift. Find it.

If you are still having trouble with this exercise, ask a friend what it is that you are really good at. Are you exceptionally responsible? Are you very organized? Are you a really good listener? Are you really creative? I bet you can trace back a gift of yours to some lesson in your life.

We live in a world of duality and opposites. Sometimes we learn love through feeling unloved. We learn to appreciate peace through war. We learn how to overcome poverty consciousness by giving away the little we have. As you grow and progress through life, you will notice how new lessons continually present themselves on your path. You have a choice: You can see these lessons as gifts, as opportunities to learn and grow in accordance with your soul's desires, or you can see these lessons as arrows piercing your heart, knocking you down, as you feel victimized.

Which will you choose?

When we realize there is nothing that is unforgivable, and that everything is a matter of perception, then we see there is only the story we keep repeating that keeps us angry, hurt and bitter, and keeps us from living a life filled with compassion, acceptance, non-judgment, joy and understanding.

> *"Forgiveness is realizing that what you thought happened, didn't."*
>
> *~ Byron Katie*

It is helpful to remember the following on your journey:

- You are not a victim in your own life plan. It is impossible.

- You are the receiver of the gift of the lessons.
- The person who brings the lessons your way is not a "bad guy," just the deliverer of the message. You are a soul having a human experience in the earth school of life.
- Each lesson is for your soul, a present, to help you on your path towards spiritual enlightenment.
- As you detach from your story, you feel more acceptance and can embrace the wisdom of the lesson.
- Feel the gratitude for a lesson well learned. You are one step closer to your soul's journey towards enlightenment.

Step by step, you walk the path towards Spiritual Enlightenment.

The path may at times be convoluted, twisted and tumultuous, and that is okay.

Embrace it.
Allow the lessons to flow gently.

~~~***~~~
~~~

Chapter 4

Forgiveness Keeps the Doctor Away

Honoring Our Health

> *"The past CANNOT provide your body with life force energy! And NOT forgiving someone is a very powerful way NOT to heal!"*
>
> *~ Caroline Myss*

As I was growing up, my mother was angry not only at my father, but at her second husband. Her anger towards my father lasted over 20 years. As an adult, I realize that by holding onto so much anger, she was really hurting herself. In recent years, she had exhibited an amazing amount of anxiety and a strong case of "poor me." My sisters and I can tell you, it was VERY STRESSFUL dealing with her, and I cannot imagine the stress of living inside her head. The world was a very scary place for my mother. It turned out she had something called "Cushing's syndrome," the result of a tumor on her pituitary gland.

Now, none of us can say for sure that stress caused this disease, but the tumor on the pituitary gland did cause her additional stress, anxiety and memory problems. The pituitary is the control center of hormones and it tells the brain to tell the body to go into fight or flight mode. As a result, cortisol was then released from the adrenal glands and pumped into her system daily. For how many years, we do not know, but we do know that when cortisol is continually pumped into your body, it affects your immune system, messes up blood sugar levels, can cause diabetes and many other life-altering illnesses.

I am sharing this story about my mother with you because you do not need to have a known physical illness for this to happen. STRESS alone causes the same bodily responses. Further, stress can settle into your body as a result of not letting go of grudges and affronts from your past. In other words, when you try stuffing your emotions or ignoring a hurt, even with spiritual intentions, your body can react as though the stressful situation is taking place right now! This is why it is so important to bring stress levels down on a regular basis. Forgiveness is one way to do this. Other ways are walking, meditation, yoga, being out in nature, aerobic exercise, making love, massage and laughing. Finding ways to relax and let go of anger and hurt regularly is imperative for good health.

At first, cortisol feels good; it is a natural pain reliever and reduces inflammation. Many of us have lifestyles that create stress and inflammation in our bodies. These stressors include sitting in traffic, worrying about money and how to pay the bills, deadlines, eating processed foods, sitting in front of computers all day, responding to the demands of others non-stop throughout the day due to technology, fear of losing jobs, homes or relationships, health issues for ourselves or loved ones, trying to please others and never feeling 'good enough'. To combat stressful lifestyle issues, including thoughts about our lives, our bodies keep producing and pumping cortisol. The body struggles to keep its glucose levels consistent, leading to weight gain, more body inflammation, immune system suppression, diabetes, depression, anxiety and various autoimmune and other diseases. A holistic approach, changing our thoughts, exercise, eating a more alkaline diet, and regular stress relief activities are necessary to maintain good health.

John Gray, author of the Men are from Mars, Women are from Venus series, says many chronic illnesses today are linked to stress and high cortisol levels. Moreover, happiness levels are directly related to lower cortisol levels! He says that because our brains are different, men and women respond to stress differently. Men literally have a larger, "fight or flight area of the brain" so they can handle stress better. In women, stress is attached to emotions and talking is what helps us lower stress levels. This is why women need to "talk" about their problems, because talking creates bonding and releases oxytocin, the "bonding" hormone. Oxytocin actually helps to lower blood pressure and cortisol levels and reduces anxiety, especially in women.

Interestingly, 'being successful' and 'taking action' helps men lower their stress levels, which is why they want to naturally 'fix' women's problems. To help women feel less stressed out, men will say "it's ok, no big deal, don't worry" which never really helps women! Men's stress comes mostly from thinking they *should* be able to repair a situation and then discover they cannot do so. However, I have learned that most men will not feel stressed when they have objectively determined that the solution to a problem is out of their control.

One of the greatest causes of stress is the simple "thought" we have. Our thoughts, like the food that comes into our bodies, can be either acidic or alkaline. The more harsh our thoughts, the more acidic they can be.[7] Where does cancer grow? That's right, in an acidic environment.[8] It logically follows that unhealthy thoughts create an unhealthy internal environment. Also, those thoughts create our external environment, since everything is born from thought. Think about it, NOTHING has ever happened, or was ever created in your life that was not FIRST a thought. So, the lesson here is that if you want to change and be happy and healthy, you must think empowering, healthy, creative, loving, and forgiving thoughts.

You are in charge of your destiny.
It starts right here,
right now, with your thoughts.

Our cells are like little microcosms of our internal universe, and they cannot be in growth and defense at the same time.[9] So it is quite a problem if our thoughts are stuck in an addictive pattern of self-abuse and destructive behavior. Have you ever felt like you just cannot find the "off" button, where your thoughts seem to automatically go round and round? I was at a Dr. Joe Dispenza[10] educational seminar where he was talking about our brain and body connection and he taught 15 minutes after animals in the wild were attacked and almost eaten, their flight and fight mode subsides. They are okay, living in the present, concentrating on the now. Humans, however, can just think about something that happened 5, 10, 20 years ago and our bodies respond as though we are in the middle of that stressful situation! Why do we keep doing this to ourselves?

It's as though we are addicted to the trauma drama and we keep tormenting ourselves over and over again!

Dr. Joe Dispenza's research shows that our bodies are literally addicted to those thoughts, and, at times, the body starts responding even before the thoughts become entrenched! He says meditation is a very useful tool because it moves us from our analytical mind into the subconscious mind, where change can take place. There is less resistance to change at that "alpha-theta" level and that is where the miracles can happen. This is where the stuck patterns of thought-emotion-body response can start to release. When you make the decision to start releasing, forgiveness is the inevitable next step.

Sarah McLean, Author of *Soul Centered: Transform Your Life in 8 Weeks with Meditation* (Hay House 2012) says "[o]ne key to being less stressed and more present is to just do whatever you're doing more slowly. Slow down on purpose."

> *"When you change the way you look at things,*
> *the things you look at change."*
> *~ Wayne Dyer*

I want to share with you something I taught in my divorce book[11] that really explains thoughts, emotions and beliefs in a simple, understandable way. YOU can change your beliefs in an instant with this simple method. In other words, you can change the STORY you make up, and release the disempowering beliefs that continue to hurt you.

This is a process called the ABC method of Managing your Attitude and I first heard of it from ISS publishing on the Internet. This is how it works:

"A" stands for the "Activating Event"

"B" stands for your "Belief System"

"C" stands for the "Consequence of the Event"

A + B + C = YOUR STORY and YOUR STORY is just made up BS (belief systems or bullshit, same thing!)

Here is a simple example:

A = you get stuck in traffic.

B = you believe that traffic is getting worse and you'll be stuck for a long time.

C = you become angry, certain expletives are said in your head or out loud and you may even find yourself banging your fist on the horn or dashboard.

After going through this pattern a few times, most people will go right from A (traffic) to C (angry), believing that the traffic jam made them angry! How can a traffic jam make you angry? It doesn't even make sense. Yet, I know you know exactly how this works! We act like little robots, as though we do not even have a choice! We skip right by B and never actually determine, choose or change our robotic belief system.

So, let's *choose* an empowering belief concerning getting stuck in traffic again, concentrating on knowing you have a choice around "B" your "Belief system."

A = you get stuck in traffic.

B = you believe you were given the gift of unexpected and extra time.

C = you listen to a tape, or plan your day or breathe and meditate and you end up feeling gratitude for the extra gift of time!

Changing your belief has a direct impact on the outcome! How you FEEL for the rest of the day can be dramatically altered by the belief you take away from any situation.

How do you use this with other areas in your life, namely forgiveness? The key is noticing the feeling of fear, hurt or anger. If that comes up, go back to "A" the "Activating Event" and process through the entire A, B, C, changing your B.

A. Name the event: My son does not call me for Mother's Day.

B. Choose what you **want** to "Believe" about the event. I could go straight to he doesn't love me, he's a selfish brat, or he simply forgot it is Mother's Day. Which belief or perspective is more empowering? I'll choose the last one; he doesn't know it is Mother's Day.

C. Consequence. If I chose one of the first two, I would most likely be hurt or angry. I would then have to eventually forgive him, and a piece of that hurt would stay to me until I released it. I would have wasted time being hurt or angry and mad at him, and creating a whole trauma-drama scene. If you are going to make something up anyway, choose an empowering story/belief, choose he did not know it was Mother's Day.

If you recognize and choose your B's (beliefs) and live from the place of understanding, acceptance, non-judgment, compassion and joy, there is nothing to forgive. Life is a bit easier that way. You put yourself in charge of responding rather than reacting to life.

> *Remember, "Beliefs are just thoughts you think over and over again."*
>
> *~ Abraham via Esther Hicks*

Mind-Body-HEART Connection

I want to take this just one step further. Let's look at the heart.

> *"The human Heart is now documented as the strongest generator of both electrical and magnetic fields in the body. Important, because we've always been taught that the brain is*

> *where all of the action is. While the brain does have an electrical and a magnetic field, they are both relatively weak compared to the Heart. The Heart is about 100,000 times stronger electrically and up to 5,000 times stronger magnetically than the brain. Important, because the physical world – as we know it – is made of those 2 fields: electrical and magnetic fields of Energy. Physics now tell us that if we can change either the magnetic field or the electrical field of the atom, we literally change that atom and its elements within our body and this world. The human Heart is designed to do BOTH."*
>
> *~ David Math, TruSparta*

What does this have to do with forgiveness? We know the brain sends messages to the body. The heart is one of the most powerful organs in the body, and it also responds to the brain's directions. It is imperative to your health to maintain good communications between the brain and the body. It's a two-way street.

An interesting study described in the *Psychological Science Journal* (March 2001) stated that those who hold grudges are more at risk of heart problems and high blood pressure than those who are naturally forgiving, and it confirms what Dr. Joe Dispenza says, that just THINKING about the situation causes higher heart rates and blood pressure! And, even after you are done 'thinking' about it, the research shows those risks are still higher!

What happens when you are stressed because you have been hurt? You put up a wall, right? You bend over backwards trying to do everything possible not to be hurt again. That includes pushing love away, trying to control everything in your life, being 'perfect.' You might not like hearing this, but fortifying a wall around you is NOT good for your health. You need to let your guard down and disassemble that wall so your body communication centers can work well.

Fortifying a wall around you
to protect yourself,
and keep yourself from being hurt,
is NOT good for your health!

We all have our stories, and most of the time, they are simply our Belief System, or BS. When that BS we make up causes us hurt, anger, bitterness or resentment, we get stressed. When we get stressed-out, unhealthy hormones are released in our system. Our acidic environment grows. When this happens, our body does not respond in a healthy way and we become ill. Regular forgiveness can relieve the initial hurt or anger and your body functions the way it was designed to function.

Numerous research projects have found that when you hold on to hurt, anger and bitterness, cortisol is continuously pumped into the body causing ill health, disease, and even cancer. Forgiveness literally reverses the effects of the stress-induced hormone cortisol, and gives the immune system a chance to repair the disease.

The Forgiveness Project, in cooperation with the Cancer Treatment Centers of America, has stated that cancer, and other life-altering diseases, can benefit from forgiveness. Many of their patients live in a state of chronic unforgiveness – a holding onto anger, hate and resentment. What they have found is that when these thoughts of unforgiveness, anger, hate and resentment are released, the immune system is enhanced tremendously. This is confirmed by Don Colbert, M.D., in his 2006 book, *Deadly Emotions: Understand the Mind-Body-Spirit Connection that can Heal or Destroy You*, says that when chronic anger is present, the body has a steady drip of the hormone cortisol. This excessive presence of cortisol can cause the immune system to become confused and to attack itself, causing auto-immune diseases. This increased level of cortisol can also contribute to diabetes, weight gain, bone loss, impaired memory and other health problems.

Forgiveness strengthens your immune system.

Research is concurring with findings that show that forgiveness can strengthen your immune system. [12] Dr. Harold Koenig in his book, *The Healing Connection* (2004), found that "[t]he research indicates those who can't get past these hurt and angry feelings of spiritual discontent may soon be in big trouble in terms of their emotional and physical health." Interestingly, Duke University Medical Center found that those who practice forgiveness experience lower levels of chronic pain and have less associated psychological problems like anger and depression than those who do not practice forgiveness.

Even the Mayo Clinic is recognizing the connection between forgiveness and health, with three forgiveness articles on their website under health. The professionals are definitely acknowledging the connections that have long been recognized by the spiritual and religious communities, that forgiveness has definite ramifications on mental, physical and spiritual well-being.

Taking Responsibility for Your Health[13]

Traditional western medicine focuses on treating symptoms rather than the root causes of illness. If we are depressed, we get a pill for depression. If we are having panic attacks, we get a pill for anxiety. If we have aches and pains, we get muscle relaxants and pain killers.

Physical or mental injury is the natural result of STUFFING emotions. When you are hurt or angry, resentful or bitter, it is usually because someone crushed your rules or expectation of how things should be. This in turn causes stress, and you already know what stress does to your body. Imagine the injury, the hurt, is like a little seed planted somewhere in your body. It hurts too much to think about the injury, so we stuff our feelings and suck it up. Well, that seed was not recognized or acknowledged by you, and it continued to grow. I cannot tell you what that seed became, but I think you can tell me. For me, the seed became a lifelong back injury, which seems to flare up whenever I repeat something that triggers the original emotional response that I stuffed to begin with. In other words, when I don't say how I feel or what I need, and instead try to please someone else.

"Illness is dis-ease. It is a final manifestation of emotional or mental difficulties. It is simply another layer of learning. "There is no fault involved. This is no punishment. This is no sign of lack of love on the part of God, your guide, or your angels. This is part of the human existence, as are the need for sleep, hot, and cold. As humanity learns to express itself on a vibrational level, illness will no longer serve a purpose and therefore will diminish."

~ Robert Schwartz,
Your Soul's Plan: Discovering the Real Meaning of the Life You Planned Before You Were Born

We now understand that what we think has profound effects on our physical well-being.

How many times has your physician asked you about your marriage? How about your stress level at work? Have you ever been asked if you are in an abusive relationship? How about whether you are harboring any resentment towards your parents, an accident you might have had years ago, or towards an ex-partner? Has your Doctor ever asked you to describe the circumstances around what happened when you injured yourself and encourage you to release the hurt and anger associated with the injury?

> *"The physician should not treat the disease, but the patient who is suffering from it."*
>
> *~ Maimonides*

I recently read about Patti Conklin, a Vibrational Mediator, who in her 20's was diagnosed with two forms of incurable and untreatable lupus. Her pain was indescribable and the medical profession gave her no hope. She was told in her dream state that color would help cure this, and she asked to see what color would cure lupus. That did not work. When she realized the lupus was caused by her lack of self worth and asked for and meditated on that color, she miraculously has not had one symptom of lupus in 25 years![14]

In addition to whatever your doctor recommends, it certainly cannot hurt to heal yourself through a regimen of healthy thoughts, forgiveness, healthy eating, meditation, massage (although massage is not recommended for certain types of cancer so check with your doctor first), connecting more with nature and exercise. In other words, start living a more alkalized lifestyle. Additionally, it would be great if you could go back and experience and FEEL the pain you felt in each incident and allow your FEELINGS and EMOTIONS to come out. Another thing you can do, if you would like, is imagine, visually and verbally, those situations resolving themselves differently, in a way where you were honored, respected, appreciated.

Please do not become one of those people who wait until one of the three D's (**Death of a loved one, Disease or Divorce)** occurs in your life before making these important life/health changes. Why do people wait for this kind of WAKE-UP call? If we know that forgiveness actually increases health, why are people reticent to forgive?

What resentment(s) are you holding onto? Why are you holding onto that anger, hurt or bitterness? Can you let go of being right to be happy? Can you let go of self-doubt, self-blame, self-guilt? Most importantly, can you let go of being wronged and instead choose to believe everything happens for a purpose, that it was meant to happen so you can heal something within yourself?

I believe most people are reticent to forgive because they wrongly believe:

1. It would let the offender off the hook if you forgive.

2. It would mean you somehow agree with or condone their bad behavior.

3. It would mean you have to naively trust that person again.

4. It means you have to have a relationship with that person.

5. It means that you are weak.

Now that YOU are clear that there is a connection between your thoughts and your stress level, what will you do about it? YOU can educate your physician that stress does affect health and that what is happening in your life is very stressful. Counselors, coaches and spiritual healers understand this. Just having someone who will listen can provide the relief you might need. It is my hope that you will COMMIT to taking responsibility for your own health by first looking at your life and see if you are holding onto any unnecessary resentment (Hint: there is NO necessary resentment!) and let it go through the forgiveness processes provided in this book. Once you are CLEAR of all past hurts, anger, fear and resentments, you'll need to continue to build your forgiveness muscle by letting go of all the small things immediately – like the person who cuts you off in traffic or the person in the grocery store line that clearly has 50 items in the 10 item only lane. Forgive and let go daily. Then, develop a routine that helps YOU keep your stress down. Aerobic exercise, meditation, healthy thinking, getting out in nature, and laughing are all good options.

~~~***~~~
~~~

Section 2:

Forgiveness in Real Life Situations

Chapter 5

Relationships: Our Greatest Teacher

Finding Wholeness and Peace through Lessons of Love and Letting Go

"Sometimes your greatest teachers in life had no idea just what they taught you. Especially those who treated you the worst.

The day you said, 'I deserve much better than this' was the day you graduated from their class."

~Unknown

One of the best ways to know ourselves is through our relationships with others. We learn how to be patient, tolerant, caring and compassionate. We learn how to express our feelings, hurts and anger. We are always learning. As I look through my own history of relationships, I can now see a pattern of growth. Okay, it's true, I was a slow learner!

I would describe my childhood relationship with my parents as me trying to figure out how to get attention. They simply were not present. Trying to get attention played out with classmates at school too, as I was pretty much ignored. I literally remember offering candy and money to other kids, hoping they would be my friend. Fortunately, things changed dramatically for me after a move to a new school and neighborhood in the fifth grade.

My early years would be characterized by patterns of 'looking for love in all the wrong places,' and 'looking for someone else to make the broken me feel whole and complete.' In the next grouping of relationships I tried to assert myself and find some self-esteem by being controlling and manipulative to get what I wanted: love and respect. Of course that did not work. I was still not whole. I would find people whose potential I could be in love with, and then spend all my energy trying to fix them. As long as I concentrated on them, I did not have to concentrate on me!

In my mid-30's, after a painful divorce, I started asking those soul searching questions: What is my purpose? Why am I here? What should I be doing with my life? If I'm not so and so's wife, who am I? There must be more to life than work, raising kids, being on community boards, and being a wife. I was certainly busy, but I was not fulfilled. Plus, I was still angry. I was hurt and humiliated, and I carried that around with me like a badge. I had many friends, yet, I felt lonely. I realized when pieces of you are missing, no one else can come along and MAKE you feel fulfilled. You need to do that for yourself. I realized it was time to work on myself before getting into the next relationship.

Let's talk about various life cycles and how they relate to relationships with others and forgiveness.

The Parent-Child Relationship

My friends Petra and Gary opened my eyes and heart to the ideas of healing the inner child within and the idea that our souls are here to have a human educational experience to further our soul's growth. The concept that we choose our lessons and the people who are major players in our lives was empowering! It took away the notion of my being a victim and taught myself that I was a co-conspirator in my own personal and spiritual growth. I started moving from a belief of "My parents and husband hurt me" to "I chose my parents and husband to learn certain lessons." These were huge lessons for me, so I better have learned something!

**Lessons are not forced upon us.
We are co-conspirators and co-designers of our personal growth experiences here on earth.**

The parent-child relationship is our first introduction to relationships on this planet. We all come in whole. We are equal and as souls do not hold onto the ego-perspective of parent-child as one being more advanced than the other. Yet as babies, we have physical and emotional needs that only adults can fulfill. This creates a duality-reality that we are seemingly unequal. As we grow, we are expected to do as we are told and we try to please our parents. Even though we might have our own inner sense of knowing what is right for us individually, we are taught (for some of us it is knocked out of us) to set aside our own beliefs and live by our parent's expectations.

Here is a simplified example of what I am talking about. Due to a lower body temperature, I am always cold and even though my children were not cold, I believed that they must be cold because I was, so, I would insist they wear a hat, gloves and coat to play outside in the winter. At the time, it made perfect sense to me. Now, looking back, it is totally illogical that I did not even allow them to determine their comfort level. I have to ask, what does that do to a child's inner sense of trusting themselves?

> *"Children understand instinctively that we are really all the same in spirit. They trust without reservation and they love without fear. They know that we are all one with the world. Their parents, on the other hand, have been hurt. They wish to keep their children safe from the disappointment and betrayal they have already experienced. So out of love and genuine parental concern, they repeatedly remind their children not to talk to strangers and warn of the horrible things that may happen if they do. By the time a child has reached first or second grade, I can see their growing reluctance to make eye contact. The innocence of childhood begins to fade and the spontaneity of the human spirit is stifled."*
>
> *~ Richard Scheinberg,*
> *Seeking Soul Mates, Spirit Guides, and Past Lives (2009)*

Here is another example, from the adult-child's perspective. During spring break, when I was in law school, I went with my father, his wife and my sisters to Disney World. I never liked rides. My father told me to take my sister on the Space Mountain roller-coaster. I did not want to go. He kept telling me that she was too young to go alone and I needed to take her. I was always trying to please him, so I gave in. I did NOT want to go. I ended up with a low-back injury and had to take my law school exams in bed. I even had to prepare for moot court on a cot in the law library. As a result of not standing up for myself, I have had about 25 years of daily back pain, including missed days at work, missed children's events, and outdoor activities, and I have spent untold amounts of money and time trying to heal.

My inner voice said no, and even though I was already an adult, on the way to becoming an attorney, I gave my power away to the authority figure in my life. In my mind, this injury was further proof that my father didn't love me. I felt like he threw me to the sharks to protect my sister. It was many years before he acknowledged my pain, and the part he played in it, but for me, it was even longer before I stopped blaming him and accepted responsibility for MY DECISION ultimately to go on that ridiculous ride.

Most importantly, I had to release blame and let it go, otherwise I would be a victim forever! Forgiving my father was a long process, maybe because I was reminded of it daily, but for me, forgiveness was like removing one layer of the onion at a time. The FEELINGS of rejection and insignificance I felt over this incident continued into my marital relationships. It was not until I could totally let go and forgive my father that I was able to find a healthy enough partner who did not trigger those feelings in me.

The process was slow. In fact, during the writing of this book, I went to visit my father and my back went out again! As with all things, this was perfect because now I am able to share with you my lesson so you can learn from my mistakes and how I realized the return of the pain ended up being another healing lesson for me. I will share more of this story with you in chapter 9.

> *"The best years of your life are the ones in which you decide your problems are your own. You don't blame them on your mother, the ecology, or the President. You realize that you control your own destiny."*
>
> *~ Albert Ellis*

At some point in my life, I will find myself in a position like many of my friends, having to care for or at least making decisions for my parents. Our roles will be reversed. Can I be a better caretaker than they were? Do I want to be? The truth is, there is still an angry little girl inside of me who isn't sure she wants to play this role. The super-responsible part of me says yes you will. The spirit in me says not to worry, there is still time and you need to do what is right for you. Writing this book is helping me as it is helping you to forgive, release, and allow the spirit of oneness to come through and guide me. I will listen.

No one is free from parental influences, even enlightened masters. The Buddhist Goddess of Compassion, Quan Yin, shares with us her challenges in one lifetime with forgiveness with her father when she chose to become a nun.

On Forgiveness and Compassion

You wish me to speak about forgiveness, and indeed this is a subject I know something about. When I was in the Earth plane I left my family and joined an order of Nuns, which displeased my Father greatly. I did not wish to displease him, but I knew that a spiritual path was the only life for me. My Father tried everything to get me to return home and when I would not he burned down the monastery. I forgave my Father for this act and later sacrificed much to save his life. Some wise people say that Forgiveness is done for the offended one. It gives you peace not to hold resentment and anger in your heart and of course this is true. Positive emotions are always healthier physically and mentally for a person and the more negative emotions you can release quickly the higher your vibration will be and also that of the whole planet. We are all connected and the more negativity that is dispelled benefits all sentient beings, not just the one.

But I say Forgiveness is also of benefit to the offender. It really does not matter whether or not they care to be forgiven. In my Father's case, he was so surprised when he discovered that it was I who saved his life that it changed him in a profound way. He became a very devout Buddhist and became kind and generous with others. To see this change in him was worth any sacrifice I made on his behalf.

Not all people will be transformed by your forgiveness. There are some that feed on the negative emotions of others. They would encourage your anger, your resentment, and your hatred. We do not encourage feeding these souls. So you see no matter what anyone has done that offended you, when you can reach a place of forgiveness in your heart all people benefit. The Hawaiian practice of Ho'oponopono[15] is encouraged as a way of being able to get to that place of being able to forgive. We do not expect you to jump right to that emotion without processing all your feelings, it is important to allow yourself to feel everything and then it can be released and is Pau, as the Hawaiians would say, finished. In this time of great transformation it is not time to procrastinate on practicing forgiveness.

Please make a list of all you feel have offended you and apply Ho'oponopono with them. You will feel better and all beings will benefit by it. Compassion is something that develops from forgiveness. If you cannot forgive others you will not be able to have compassion for them. First I learned forgiveness, humility, empathy and then compassion came.

Quan Yin,
Channeled through Debbie Dehm
www.CompassionateHealing.biz

Forgiveness leads to self-empowerment and a feeling of self-confidence. It is comforting to know that although I can be hurt, I can recover as a stronger and healthier me. This is a much better place from which to have fulfilling relationships.

Work Relationships

Although this chapter primarily addresses love and family relationships, I want to touch briefly on work relationships. The truth is, as adults, we sometimes spend more awake hours in our days with people at school or work, out there in the world, than we do with our family members. In addition to the time we spend with them, we are interdependent with these people for our livelihood, our finances and our social contacts.

We live in an era where automation is more valued than people and many people have lost their worker/ management status due to automation. Who are you if you are not your profession? How do you respect yourself when you cannot support yourself or your family? The stress of keeping a job has now been added to the stress of everyday working and including getting along with others, your boss, your co-workers. Sometimes we are asked to do things that are against our better judgment, and that puts additional stress on our systems.

As I write this, I can literally feel my shoulders rise and start to tighten. You might be aware that stress from work shows up in your shoulders, back, headaches. It is so important for us to remember that we are all one, even with our co-workers. We need to remember that we also planned our work issues, and our financial issues. Struggling to make decisions about how to pay bills, which bills get paid, bankruptcy, foreclosure, walking away from a job for our health, etc. are all lessons we have given ourselves to overcome. Oh, that's right, take a deep breath and allow your shoulders to relax as you remember, this is just one of those growth lessons.

Lessons in Developing Love Partnerships

We all make assumptions and sometimes those assumptions wreak havoc on our thoughts, beliefs and actions. They can literally destroy relationships. My wonderful coach Trudy taught me this lesson of perspectives, and I want to teach it to you.

Take an incident that happened to you, where you were hurt. Typically, you would make an assumption that is disempowering, in other words, you would believe the worst. Instead, name up to a half dozen things it could mean, and since it is all made up anyway, choose the most empowering perspective to believe.

I'll give you an example. When I first met my husband Kevin, I told him I definitely did not want to get remarried, which was the honest truth at the time. However, after a few months together, I knew I wanted to marry him. I KNEW he was the one for me! He had never been married and he did not want to get married. Here is what I told myself: "He doesn't think I'm good enough for him," and, with my mother's urging, "Why should he buy the cow when he gets the milk for free?" I was devastated and hurt and despondent and confused. I KNEW he loved me, I KNEW it. So why wouldn't he want to get married? Then there was all the analysis and discussions over why I felt like I wanted to be married. Couldn't we just be together and enjoy what we had. Why was I being so needy?

If I had someone work with me on perspectives, this is what it could have looked like:

1. **He doesn't love me.**
2. **He is scared of losing his freedom.**
3. **He doesn't want the responsibility that goes along with marriage.**
4. **We are so happy together. Enjoy what we have.**
5. **If I stop pushing, it would allow him space to make up his own mind.**
6. **If I really want to be married, I should go be with someone else.**
7. **Stop trying to change who he is.**
8. **You don't need marriage to experience love.**
9. **Marriage has no guarantees.**
10. **Everyday, experience his love and love him back and in time, it will work itself out.**
11. **At age 45, a man who has never been married is not going to get married. Give it up.**
12. **It is time to love yourself and stop looking for love from others.**

Of course, on some level, I understood all of this and at various times during our relationship, all these thoughts did cross my mind. However, what I didn't do was pick the most empowering ones. Instead, I constantly chose the most victimizing ones. I focused on my mother's cow analogy and the one where I wasn't good enough. We even broke up twice and I dated others. He loved me so much that he didn't want me to be unhappy and would rather me be with someone else than be unhappy. I have come to recognize that a man who truly loves a woman wants nothing more than to see her happy.

My Ah-ha lesson: During our last break-up, I left the country with another man to go to Costa Rica to write a book. That didn't last long and we broke up within a couple of weeks. Kevin and I were still in contact while I was in Costa Rica and during this time, I really learned to love myself and became more independent. I knew if Kevin did not want me back, I would be OK. I was learning to love myself and was in fact very happy with my own company. I was gaining strength and self-confidence.

When I moved back to the States, Kevin and I started living together and within 18 months we married. What happened? I believe Kevin was an impetus for my soul's growth. He had to break up with me so I could find myself. I believe he could have married me at any time but I needed this piece of soul integration – needing to focus more on my own relationship with myself, and with God. I needed to trust myself. If we had gotten married earlier, I would have been dependent on him for my happiness and probably would have repeated past cycles. Now I was able to move forward.

It was the energy of finding my own self love that allowed this partnership to manifest in this lifetime. Now, I try to remember to choose the most (self) loving answer to all my questions regarding relationships and forgiveness. This healed past cycles, put an end to unhealthy patterns and moved me forward.

I also want to add here that with my own discovery of self love, came the forgiveness of my father. I was no longer a victim. I let go of those rejection and unwanted feelings. Without those core beliefs of mine, perhaps I released the entire vibration of "rejection" from my system and Kevin was able to align himself to me without being the impetus for my healing.

I just saw this same scenario played out on the news media about singers Rihanna and Chris Brown. Three years earlier, he seriously beat her up. She said she was able to forgive him after she found peace with her father! I believe we keep attracting relationships into our lives to heal our first, primary childhood parental issues. Once that primary relationship is healed, we can choose better, healthier relationship partners.

I say all of this for you who believe that you'll never love again, it is there. My advice? Become the person you want to be in order to meet the person you WANT. If you are still looking for someone to complete you, you'll find another half-person. Two half people never make a whole; they just make broken pieces. However, two wholes truly do make one whole, healthy dynamic team.

Forgiveness and Divorce

There is an amazing gift that comes with the ending of a marriage. People rarely see it that way. They see the tragedy, the loss, the dying dreams, the dying hopes and dreams that fade away. If they have children, they lose the dream of something called "family," something they considered to be their safety net, their stability.

The gifts that come with divorce typically focus on personal and spiritual self growth. For many, we start asking the vital questions, "Who am I?" "What is my life purpose?" or "Why did this happen to me?"

Susan explains the pain and the beauty of Divorce in her story:

> *The practice of forgiveness is simple when life coasts easily forward and according to plan. The broken dish, the forgotten birthday, the insensitive words spoken are generously dismissed and forgotten. Accordingly, big hiccups in life ask for greater fortitude and surrender. My marriage was that heat-seeking hiccup aimed for collision with almost all my non-negotiables: untreated addiction, infidelity, abuse. It was a tumultuous time of growing up into myself; growing pains that accelerated through times of shock, loss and denial, while at other times meandering through tenderness, love and reconciliation. I was a reluctant and stubborn student of my own transformation, hanging so tightly onto the dream that my whole life became clenched and unbending. It*

was only then that I could shatter so completely that forgiveness had a place to grow.

Forgiving my husband turned out to be the easier part. Forgiving myself was where I met my inner tyrant who tempted me to stay in shame and self-flagellation. Regret bobbed around my feet, taunting me with the what-ifs and should-haves. What if I had loved him better? What if I had been more of this and less of that? What if I had been different and better than who I am?

So I ran. I ran miles of trails through sinewy, shedding madrone trees, towering evergreens, blackberry bushes that left stripes of welts down my legs. I splashed through creeks, scrambled up roots, gasped up hills where the clouds blanketed the valley below like a thunderous, rolling ocean. The sorrow in my heart became breath through my lungs and the woods a healing refuge. One day as I sprinted along a trail groomed with cedar chips and mulch, my foot caught beneath me and I fell. I fell directly on my face without any mid-air aerobics or attempts to catch myself with my hands. Face down in the dirt, unmoving, I thought, "Enough. It's time to get up." Suffering, I realized, required a lot of energy; especially the self-inflicted kind. I wanted my life back, even though I no longer had a vision of what that was. I felt a stir of excitement. What if my life was in the process of revealing itself to me, and all I had to do was get up, appreciate the woman I was, and believe in my own transcendence?

Forgiveness crept in slowly in the dawn of dark nights. It stole past the regrets and made gentle the tyrant. Forgiveness became the absence of fear, the absence of regrets, the absence of an attachment to how things should have been. Forgiveness became the absence of thought forms that flapped around my head like kites in a storm, pulling at the expression of my truest self. And in time, forgiveness became receiving goodness again, allowing it to percolate within me, allowing it to flow outward and connect me to others. This is the final asana, the state of grace that I've learned to hold onto as life ambles forward, gloriously messy and most certainly not according to plan.

Susan Shammel,
Ashland, Oregon

Adultery

No discussion of relationships and forgiveness can be complete without discussing adultery. Adultery leaves us feeling raw, used, and foolish. It ignites those core worthiness issues of "not good enough" begging the question, "What is wrong with me?" When I understood the extent of my ex-husband's cheating, the devastation was immense. As a family law attorney, I honestly judged others, and did not believe that they did not know their spouse was having an affair. The truth is I had no idea! Of course looking back, I can see signs, but at the time I trusted my husband and had no reason to not trust him.

I don't blame myself for being innocent or naïve anymore. Trust is a good thing, pure and beautiful. Although it was easy to put up walls of protection and not trust, I had to make a conscious choice to NOT build those walls. I had to learn to trust myself and know I could and would handle whatever comes my way!

The pervasive pain caused by cheating goes deep, and it seems only forgiveness can allow for peace. It is easy to become obsessed with it, trying to understand how this could happen. Beating yourself up for not being good enough. Judy's story is a clear example of how we can go from being gripped by the tragedy of cheating, to the peace that comes from acceptance, release, and forgiveness:

Judy's Story:

It happened again that night just as it had so many nights over the past weeks, months. I'd doze and then awaken to scattered thoughts: "How dare she go after him! How could she do that? What kind of a woman does that?" The rage would bubble up. The alarm rings and I realized I'd spent most of the night chasing those thoughts. This particular morning I struggled to face the day with less than two hours sleep when I got in the car to drive the hour and half commute to work. As my car crept along through heavy traffic the story played through my mind.

Reunited with a love from college we had been living together for a couple of years when his consulting business slowed and he began teaching high school science. It was an adjustment for him from working with corporations to teenagers but he enjoyed it and had met several teachers there who were very helpful. One in particular seemed to always be there when he needed assistance. I met her. She was sweet and friendly. Once she even sat in our living room commenting on how cute a couple he and I were. Several months later, I sat in that same living room with my partner hearing how he had fallen in love with this woman. Life changed. We lived separately under the same roof until he moved out. Far from lovers, the foundation of friendship carried us forward. I even found myself helping him pack his things for his move months later.

It was then that I found the poem she had written for him. It told of how she had fallen for him the very first day they met, how she had pursued him actively despite knowing he was in a committed relationship. She elaborated the details of her love and emotions. Feelings of anger and betrayal coursed through me, now directed at her. These same feelings raged through my thoughts and disturbed my sleep.

As I drove through rush hour traffic, reviewing the "facts", the fatigue and weariness hung heavily on me. I struggled to keep my eyes open and focused on the cars and the road. The anger and rage had wreaked havoc on me. "I'll bet she slept through the night and is feeling great this morning." It dawned on me. The anger I had toward her caused her no harm, no sleepless nights. I was the one being hurt with the rage. I was suffering. Suddenly the rage left me. I felt a great weight lifted. My head cleared and all thoughts of anger were gone. She had acted thoughtlessly from her emotions and meant me no harm. I was responsible for my suffering. In that moment, I chose to forgive her and forgive myself.

Judy Chiger, MD, PhD
www.drjudychiger.com

You might have already noted this, but Judy is a doctor and I was a lawyer when the cheating took place. We are not dummies! When working with people who are beating themselves up, searching for the answer to WHY, I point out that many successful, beautiful women like Actress Sandra Bullock, model Elin Nordegren, and the smart, savvy, Journalist Maria Shriver, wife of Arnold Schwarzenegger, all experienced the same thing! Yes, even they ask, "Why, what's wrong with me? Why wasn't I enough?" The hurt runs deep in all of us. Men as well are emotionally devastated when their partners cheat on them, their self-esteem and self-confidence take a beating too.

Even in these situations it is imperative to remember that there is no real bad guy/good guy. It is never black and white. It is easier to think in terms of black and white, good or bad, right or wrong when someone breaks our rules or societal rules by which we live. It is easy to blame the person who broke the rules. But, if we continue to blame that person, we remain the victim. If we continue to blame that person, we never have to take personal responsibility and learn from the experience. Remember my story with my first husband. If I continued to blame him, I would not have faced my own unhealthy relationship demons of being too controlling, not feeling good enough, and worrying about rejection and abandonment. Now I know, I can handle whatever comes my way, and I have healthier boundaries and self-esteem.

Abuse

Of course, it would be easy to discuss abuse, physical, verbal or emotional abuse in the following chapter on forgiving the unforgivable. However, I think it is appropriate here, as most abuse does take place within the family unit. The ones we trust the most, the ones who are entrusted to protect and care for us, are in a position to abuse. In my book, *Freedom from Abuse: Finding Yourself Again* (2009), I discuss the eerie similarities between the abuser and the victim, which partially explains why and how we attract each other. In some cases, partners came from abusive backgrounds and truly have to learn that they deserve NOT to be abused. There is great personal growth in experiencing the escaping and surviving of domestic abuse. It is truly life altering.

In this particular story, we are talking about spousal abuse, where an adult without many outside resources has to find the strength and the courage to leave her relationship, even if it means losing her children.[16] Michele Penn shares her story and the amazing transformation she was able to make once she followed through with the decision to gain her freedom and find herself again.

Michele's Story:

My book with Eckhart Tolle, "Peace in the Present Moment," is the result of my journey to consciousness.

My ex-husband verbally abused my children and me for years. He eventually threatened to kill me in an emotionally violent rage. I can forgive him today because that experience was the catalyst that fueled my desire for spiritual knowledge. I left him and instead of losing my life, I found it! I heard Oprah say "Forgiveness is letting go of the hope that the past could be any different." And by forgiving him as well as myself, I was set free. I discovered strength in myself that I didn't even know I had.

I became aware of flowers after I truly forgave the unforgivable. Where had they been all my life? Why had I not seen them before? I was being awakened to their beauty by my ability to forgive. I was captivated by their inner beauty, the soul of the flower and had an intense desire to capture that moment for others. I felt oneness with source. The gifts of this forgiveness journey continue every day of my life.

My inspiration of flowers, and reading "A New Earth" by Eckhart Tolle, intensified the process of awakening for me. Interestingly, the first chapter was called "The Flowering of Human Consciousness" and while I was reading it I felt as if Eckhart was in my head. He touched my soul with his words. Eckhart says that "seeing beauty in a flower could awaken humans, however briefly, to the beauty that is an essential part of their own inner most being, their true nature." I knew this! Flowers had AWAKENED ME!

I then had an inspired thought. I KNEW that Eckhart would connect with my flowers as profoundly as I connected with his words. I KNEW we were going to do a book together. I designed a mock up book, with my photos and his quotes from "A New Earth." Eckhart wanted Byron Katie (another one of my mentors) to also be a part of this beautiful journey! Yes, there is a story, but suffice it to say, "Peace in the Present Moment" is now a reality.

I continue to manifest amazing things into my life, the man of my dreams and the power of the present moment. I am living the life I always imagined.

Michelle Penn
www.PeaceInThePresentMoment.net

You might question, should abuse be forgiven. Of course, remember, it has nothing to do with the abuser; it is 100% about the person who was hurt and injured. They can not move forward with peace if they are angry and blaming, because if they are, they remain victimized forever. You will read more about forgiving the unforgivable in the next chapter.

Parental Alienation

As a divorce attorney, I've seen it all, but the greatest pain a parent can suffer is to lose their child, especially when they are a really good parent. Using the children to punish the other parent is not unfamiliar in the family court arena, but for the parent, it can be devastating. And the emotional harm it causes children can last their entire lifetime.

I have to share with you a painfully sad story as told by my friend Barry. This story could certainly go into the "unforgivable chapter" yet I believe it happens frequently enough that you just might be able to relate to this story.

At the time of the initial event my son was nearly five years old. We had recently concluded what seemed like an amazing weekend of fun and games, rough housing, hiking in the woods, pretend cops and robbers, and a made up fishing game. The imagination of a small child is amazing. It is funny how perception works, when one person sees something completely different than the other person. Often, we only see what we wish to see.

During the exchange drop off with our son on a bright and sunny afternoon in April of 2009, I decided for whatever unconscious reason to give into a deliciously charged question from my ex-wife. We had been sharing the negative energy for a long time now. This moment was a catalyst in our relationship. What made me do it? Ego, ignorance, unawareness, spite, hatefulness, revenge . . . to name a few. Definitely not Love. What was the question? My ex-wife asked me if I had tied him up and handcuffed him . . . . My cynical response, "Oh yeah! You know me." This was true as we did play some really fun games that weekend with a pair of toy handcuffs and the soft fuzzy waist band for catching fish. Unfortunately, that was all she needed to hear.

As I waved good bye to my son I had no idea what was about to transpire in the next ten months. That following week I was visited by two police officers inquiring about physically abusing my son. This prompted a massive investigation and I was only allowed to visit my son at the court house in a special visitation center. All of the visits with him were positive and loving. At the end of each visit he would give me a hug and tell me he loved me. I would cry the entire car ride home. It was both emotionally painful and psychologically maddening. Initially these accusations were found to be falsified, but that was not the end.

As the months went on my son's health, behavior and attitude began to deteriorate in his home environment under his mother's care. He began to act out and talk back to his mother. He was not listening to directions or following simple rules. He started peeing behind his bed and hiding objects like forks and tweezers in various places around the house. After she lost leverage with the physical abuse charges, she then decided to file sexual abuse charges, further blaming me for his behavior under her care. It was like having a bomb dropped on me. I could not believe someone would accuse another person of molesting a small child. And their own child for that matter! After more positive and loving visits with him at the visitation center the court decided to terminate the visits because his behavior became so outrageous at his mothers home. The court could not make heads or tails of what was going on. To this day I vividly remember receiving the phone call from the court visitation center about the termination of the visits with my son. Upon receiving the message I collapsed to the ground in shock. I could not believe this was happening and I did not know what I could do to help my son. I felt completely helpless. I did not sleep for days. It was beyond maddening. All I could do was let go of the fact that I had no control of the situation. Then ever so slowly I began to realize that what I did have control of was my ability to react to the events taking place. This was an illuminating revelation at the time.

After the last visit I did not visit or speak to my son for another six months. During this time period I began to go through the most rapid psychological transformation I am aware of to date. My whole world was flipped and I was blown wide open. I became silent like a monk and yet in this silence I found something more amazing than I could comprehend at the time. Forgiveness.

Because the sexual abuse charges were so severe this prompted both me and my ex-wife to take court ordered criminal forensic profile tests to determine who was a liar. At this point in the case I was informed that my son was having such a hard time under her care that they were considering placing him in a mental hospital for children. In moments like that you begin to question everything you ever knew about life and your experience to date. The amount of energy that would surge through my body at times was scary. I was so furious with her and this scenario that I wanted to tie her up behind my car and drag her down the highway until there was nothing left.

The forensic test was yet another grueling aspect of this experience that I will never forget. Over twelve hours of questions and talking to a specially trained psychologist for this type of evaluation. I even had to pay the $3,500 out of my own pocket.

Then came the breaking news after months of testing and waiting. It was lucky my son had not been committed to the mental hospital. The forensic report came back that my ex-wife was mentally unstable and that the recommendation from the psychologist who issued the forensic tests was to have my son removed from her immediately and placed under my care in my household. I could not believe it at the time. It was almost too good to be true! I remember seeing him for the first time in after six months. He looked like a zombie. All I could do was embrace him and cry. It took about three months to help him get re-acquainted with a healthy lifestyle and loving household again. Today he thrives under my care and is one of the happiest children you will ever meet!

Looking back I still would not change any of it. It was perfect. Why? Because when you start to ask questions like, "Why would anyone do this to me?" or "Why is this happening to me?", you begin to realize that no matter what anyone ever does to you the only thing you can control is how you react. That's it. That's all anyone can ever do. And when you get to that place, you realize people aren't actually taking actions against you, and that it has nothing to do with you at all. You are simply a match in some way to the expression of emotions and feelings they have inside of them. You learn to forgive them because you then realize that they are suffering so deeply and do not know how to cope and dispel the pain they continue to re-experience inside of themselves. In my ex-wife's case she was molested as a small child and has never recovered from that experience. She projected these feelings of pain towards me as an attempt to "fix" everything she experienced as a child using our five year old son at the time as leverage.

Now two and a half years later I wish her nothing but the biggest and brightest happiness she can find. What I learned about reacting to a situation and about how to forgive are priceless life lessons. Forgiveness cleans the wounds and allows you to move forward with life. It begins the healing process. Forgive yourself for choices you have made that you blame yourself for or felt you could not control. Then forgive the other person for whatever they have done to you or towards you. Forgiveness is one of the most amazing gifts you can give in Life.

Barry Costa
www.BarryCosta.com

As you can see, relationships are the perfect vehicles for personal growth. Whether it's with your parents, children, extended family, a love-partnership, or even co-workers, professionals, community leaders or politicians, we are often pushed to our limits! When relationships are good, we are in heaven. When they are bad, they can destroy our spirit and our joy. Madly in love can, in a moment, turn into breach of trust and the pain of loss, rejection, and abandonment. Barry's triumph over what could have been a disastrous outcome with the use of forgiveness is a perfect example of a human embracing his soul's lessons.

Forgiving Loved Ones
After They have Passed Over

As it turns out, not everyone is complete and satisfied with their relationships while they are alive and their lessons with their loved one, the one who has caused them so much pain, or the one to whom they have inflicted pain. The lessons continue even after death.

Sometimes, it is easier to forgive after death, as the daily pain has subsided. When something is truly in the past, when the offense can no longer continue, it is easier to forgive.

Ascended Master, Djwhal Khul, has blessed us with a perspective on the importance of forgiving, even after one party has passed over. Of course, since we know we are spirit having a human experience, and our human experiences are designed for the purpose of our soul's growth, then it makes perfect sense to continue our forgiveness lessons after someone has passed over.

'Forgiveness After Death'

A channeled perspective by Ascended Master Djwhal Khul, also known as The Tibetan.

Djwhal Khul here, Tashi delek, a very warm Tibetan greeting to you. Tashi delek is recognizing the happy auspicious already enlightened being in you. In other words, we greet each other soul to soul, light to light.

About forgiveness. *Forgiveness is often misunderstood. Unfortunately, it is not something that is well practiced in society. To quote Buddha, 'remembering a wrong is like carrying a burden on the mind.'*

Most people carry a grudge or are mad about something in the past. They worry that it will repeat again in the future so they keep their defenses up. Oftentimes, this is a conscious or unconscious excuse to punish someone else. Sometimes they will make a whole family suffer for a divorce that occurred earlier or an affair that occurred at some time. Maybe it is over a child who got injured or handicapped in some way. There are all kinds of ways that plays out including country to country, religion to religion, and other forms due to not letting go of toxic beliefs.

When someone is in the midst of the pain of not being able to forgive, it is difficult for them to see that they are the one generating the pain and that they are also punishing themselves. It seems as though it is the person outside of them or the neighbor or any other trigger. It seems like the problem is out there and 'they' need to change.

In personal and spiritual growth it is said that the journey is always about the self. It begins with self and it ends with self. Change must then come from inside and not from anywhere outside.

What Happens at Death? *At the moment of passing, the spirit leaves the body and begins the process of the Bardo. If you want to read "The Tibetan Book of the Dead", that would have much more material. I've also created a spirituality article[17] on "The Bardo" which has been quite popular. You could review that for a little bit more information.*

When one leaves the embodiment, one of the first things that happens is that they realize they've done this many times before. It is a familiar process. If it was a long illness or other lengthy passing, one sometimes looks back and wonders why there were so attached and afraid to die. This is because the beliefs that were accumulated in the lifetime are now gone.

What happens is one transitions from a tiny, tiny pinpoint of existence to the expanded full consciousness of real self. It is a realization that the whole life, the whole world, and what seemed to be a vast universe, was just a tiny portion of who they really are and who we as a collective consciousness really are.

Upon death, one is released from limited perception and trying to compact self into a seemingly complex existence. It is literally like getting out of self-imposed prison. Expansion into Oneness is experienced.

In the Tibetan way of the Bardo, one has about three days' earth time in which they do a lot of shamanic journeying. There is a lifetime review for karma, good and bad, with assessment of causes and effects upon self and others. You can make amends in that three-day window and enlightenment may also be achieved.

That is when one might realize for example 'Oh my goodness, I held that grudge against my sister-in-law for 40 years and it was such a silly thing to maintain.' Then one can forgive self for tying their own energy up in a negative way.

Sometimes they energetically visit the sister-in-law and communicate something like 'I really am sorry I put both of us and all others involved through all that suffering. Will you forgive me for not being able to see the bigger picture?'

They forgive the other person symbolically more so than literally because it really isn't about forgiving the other person. It's about forgiving self, first and foremost. It is easy to realize this in the expanded state of consciousness.

Oftentimes, family and loved ones will not see or sense the recently departed around much during the Bardo period. There are exceptions to this, of course. Usually loved ones feel like the one who left is gone permanently at first, especially if their beliefs about death say so. They may be contacted through meaningful dreams or synchronicities if that is the case.

In that initial three-day period, one is really very busy with the review process. Sometimes they make contact to let others know they passed and then go into the Bardo. They might also visit with glee just after the Bardo. It is common for the spirit to be present at their own celebration of life.

Life after Death. *After the Bardo, one chooses their next path of existence as an eternal being. Some come back in spirit form to protect small children or other loved ones. Some of the very elderly when they leave their bodies learn computers and advanced technology on the other side. It seems so simple and so in sync with Creation from the other side.*

One can work with the angelic realms too. Some become angels of death and help others pass when it's their time. Some help the animal kingdoms get their newborns strong quickly to survive in the wild and help the ailing ones make their transition quickly and easily. There are a lot of jobs to choose once one gets to the other side.

Ninety-nine percent of the time the ones who have transitioned are completely at peace and glad that they have been freed from the compacted existence they were in. They are very, very happy on the other side. And that is the goal, to achieve happiness. They show up in dreams or wakened states conveying that they are happy and wish happiness for others. The purpose of all life in the Tibetan way is to be happy.

If they show up unhappy, it could be that ceremony or prayer is needed to free the soul. Usually, negative images are the survivor's projected memories and not the accurate state of the being on the other side. There are exceptions to this therefore it would be wise to find out which one is true so that help may be received.

Forgiveness for the Surviving. *What happens to the person who's still embodied and part of this forgiveness loop is oftentimes very interesting. Let's say the person who left was a suicide or there is some other perception of them having done it to themselves. Let's say it's perceived they took their life in some way by neglecting their own physical body or driving dangerously or doing drugs or whatever.*

The people left behind oftentimes carry guilt or regret. They ask 'What should I have done?' or 'What could I have done?' They beat themselves up with shame and blame until they find help out of the pattern. What I would say compassionately is that this is eternity. It is not all about that one lifetime. There is a much bigger plan.

The person left behind harboring the guilt often has more work to do. Sometimes they will be understandably angry at the person who left their body. We sometimes refer to this as 'dropping the body' because we see all spirits as still here. People don't go away. The tangible form is not there anymore but the spirit is ever-present. It cannot be extinguished, it lives forever. We are literally eternal.

You might even feel in this incarnation that you are an old soul recycled numerous times and you're not done being recycled yet. You may have the sense that you and others you know will be back in some form over and over playing different roles with each other. This is truth.

Guilt is anger turned inward. It is very harmful to the self. Rather than trying to forgive the person who is gone, focus inward. Ask how can I forgive myself? And do I need to forgive myself or do I just need to say 'I accept what happened, it is what it is'? We know ultimately that we have no control over others. We try to save them out of instinct or to perhaps buy some time for a healing process. In the end, they decide what they want and need for the soul's growth.

Some of those who are incarnate here are miserable yet want to make physical existence work. They might look toward drug therapies or medicate with alcohol or extreme sports or try any other means to find a way of being in this world that might work for them at least temporarily. If they're truly not happy, they will find a way to get out of the incarnation sooner or later, one way or another. We bless these souls for being brave as they work in a constant upstream struggle.

In rare cases, at the end of that three-day Bardo, they jump right back into another body. Usually they wait months or decades in earth time staying in the ethers and focusing on retaining the ability to stay in a blissful state before they reincarnate. Often, a very good painter will come back and be a painter again. Or one who invents technology will come back and invent technology again. Singers and songwriters come back frequently now and some start very young in the body. Their talent is apparent and they will bring back classic works of art as well as marvels of healing technology.

This is very important to know . . . those who are already on the other side have forgiven you. They're not holding anything. They can't really hold grudges. There is the exception of a very few disincarnate spirits that you might call 'ghosts' who haunt. It is possible to get trapped in the astral plane and still think you're an individual entity instead of the vast consciousness that you are in truth. These spirits can be freed by ceremony. Usually we wait until they say 'Okay, I'm tired of this, I'd like to try something else' and then we help them into the light from the other side.

If someone is visiting you in that way, ask them what they want. They want something. They either want closure or just someone to listen to them. They maybe want to be appreciated or they want to say good-bye. They're not getting something that they need, essentially. But that's very, very rare. Most of the time death is a release, then bliss, and then remembering 'Oh yes, I've done this over and over. I'm going to review my life now, clear up any loose ends, and look at all the good I have done in the world. Then I'll decide what I'll do next.'

During that three-day time period, it's the best time to put a lot of love into that person's spirit. Rather than thinking 'What went wrong?' sing about love or chant Om for peace. You want to celebrate their spirit and send them volumes of love, as much as you can possibly send. That will assist them in their process and they can reach enlightenment as a result of the love and peace directed to them during the Bardo period and also afterward at any time. It is never too late.

Maybe annually on their birthday celebrate them again. Someone you deeply love, you naturally want to celebrate. You could celebrate their passing and their transition to enlightenment or their birthday, anniversary, or any other special occasions. Think of their spirit as ever present and very loving.

You can also ask them to help you. 'I'm concerned about making a career move. Can you give me some guidance from the other side?' Remember they can see the bigger picture. It is wise to maintain a good and mutually beneficial relationship. You may get the answers in your dreams or indirectly on the physical plane, such as an article or opportunity shows up at just the right moment.

To create forgiveness after death, go within and handle it from within. From a spiritual perspective, it's not necessary to formally sit down face to face in body or commune with spirit and say 'I forgive you. Will you forgive me?' Forgiveness is done solely from within.

Forgiveness in Life. *Some people, depending on their personality, certainly do appreciate an apology or an acknowledgment. In the moment or soon after are the best times. Generally it's kind of offensive to say 'By the way, I forgive you for what you did to me when we were 12.' That is actually bringing, or dragging, the past into the present moment. It is an indicator that it is not forgotten and not forgiven.*

When we forgive internally and then sense the other person may still be thinking about it, we can make light of it. 'Remember when you pushed me in the swimming pool and I busted my chin open at 12? Weren't we crazy, wild, indestructible children?' That communicates all is forgiven. The other person does not have to keep looking at the scar and regretting the moment. They may express their sorrow, verbally or non-verbally, and they may not.

Find many ways to communicate forgiveness, especially non-verbally and through the power of love. It is not necessary to involve another person or persons in a process they might not appreciate. You will spare much pain for yourself and for others when you let go and free yourself from the past. Forgiveness is an inside job and always will be.

Divine love is the absence of fear and brings us to the state of Oneness. Love yourself deeply so that you can love everyone and everything deeply.

As always, thank you and my love to you.

Djwhal Khul
Channeled through Rev. Terri Newlon
www.TerriNewlon.com

Relationships are fabulous healing tools. Even our great earth masters, Jeshua and Buddha, and more recently, Gandhi and King, ended up becoming role models for humbleness and humility through the relationships with others. Were they not tormented, questioned and abused? Each one suffered at the hands of others, they were humiliated by others. Were they humble before or did this humiliation make them humble? I can say for sure in my own relationship, I was humiliated, I felt like a fool and it made me more humble and more compassionate towards others. I believe I am a better person as a result of the humiliation I endured.

"Beginnings are often disguised as painful endings."

Oh, if we could only remember that we are spirit, that God is inside each of us, that we are only here for a short time in this earth school, and that these are only lessons, how much easier our lives would be!

~~~***~~~
~~~

Living with Forgiveness Process

This process can be remembered by the ARGG – think of a dog growling ARGG with a rope in its mouth and you'll remember the process and be able to practice it over and over again.

Acknowledgment and **A**cceptance, **R**esponsibility, **G**ifts, and **G**ratitude

Step 1. Acknowledgment and Acceptance: Living with forgiveness doesn't mean being perfect, and it doesn't mean we are just oh so spiritual, so enlightened. It means we recognize our humanness; we recognize and accept our own personal traumas. Where do we beat ourselves up? Where do we blame others for our hurts? Our goal is to recognize when we are feeling hurt, anger, bitterness or resentment.

Acknowledge it. Feel the feelings, for they are real. Then, do a perspectives exercise. Choose a more empowering perspective if you can. Sometimes the truth is we are just not ready to forgive or to accept what happened. Keep revisiting it because you will be ready.

I did have to learn to forgive my ex-husband. I want to show you how I did it and how you can do it using this "Living with Forgiveness Process." Feel free to copy!

> *Lori's situation: Step 1.* Acknowledgment and Acceptance: My first husband cheated on me and we chose not to stay together. The family unit will never be the same.
>
> (Note: This is as simple as saying, what is the reality of the situation?)

Step 2. Personal Responsibility: If someone cheats on you, remember, they acted and did something. HOW it affects YOU is entirely your choice, your decision. The act itself is neutral. You can give it any feeling you want – it can be neutral or painful to you. Do you want to forgive them? Do you want to look at your part in the relationship? Do you choose to take a hard look at your piece in this situation to help you grow both personally and spiritually? Most important, what did you do that allowed this to happen?

> *Lori's situation: Step 2.* My first husband cheated. What I did not know until I took real time for self-reflection was that I was controlling in my relationship with him and so

emasculating to him, that he did not feel like a man. Although I can't say for sure what was in his mind, my inner guidance tells me that he was looking for someone else to admire and respect him, because he was not getting it from me. My ego self says, he wanted to punish me for being such a bitch. My spirit says he needed to feel appreciated and I was not giving him this. Does this mean what he did was okay? No, of course not. It does mean that I have been given a great learning lesson. I was behaving more like a mother than a wife to him. My behavior does not excuse his behavior. Each partner in a relationship has the responsibility to speak up. It is best, obviously, to either work it out or leave in an honorable, honest way.

Taking responsibility for my piece does NOT mean I have to trust him. It does NOT mean what he did is okay. It does NOT mean I condone his behavior. It only means that I have to acknowledge the part that is my responsibility.

Step 3. Finding the Gift: There are many places to discover the gift in all aspects of relationships. It is often found in the personal responsibility aspect or in the spiritual aspect after the relationship is over and we focus on our own personal growth. What we want is to learn about *ourselves* and see lessons beyond the obvious. Many true lessons are about the discovery of self-love and raising self-esteem. Lessons and answers come when we start asking questions such as "What is my purpose here in this relationship?" If nothing else ever happens in your life, aren't these lessons alone just amazing gifts?

Many people will go to the fall-back, "my kids are my gift from this relationship!" Please go deeper than that, look deeper, at yourself, for yourself.

> *Lori's situation: Step 3.* Of course I love and adore my children and am glad they are in my life. For me, going through the lessons of Divorce, I was truly blessed to learn to deal with my own control issues and did the hard work I needed to do to make some very serious changes in my personality. Underlying control was my own fear of being rejected or abandoned. I learned that the control aspect of my relationship was partially to insure that I was not left. The opposite happened. Of course I attracted the very thing I feared the most! Because of this lesson, I learned to treat my current husband as a spouse, not as a mother. And if I do slip, he tells me!
>
> Yes, there are more gifts from my first marriage and divorce. I started on a spiritual path, asking those big questions – "Who am I?" "What is my life purpose?" and "Why are we here?" I discovered that I am a natural born teacher, coach, mediator and spiritual guide. I started on a path of self love and learned to get in touch with my own intuition. I live an exciting, fun-filled life, having helped many people, and can honestly say I am proud of what I have accomplished. I was not this person in my first marriage.

Step 4. Gratitude: Look at your life lessons and acknowledge gratitude for the experience. By feeling gratitude for the lesson, the gift of the experience opens before you. When we accept the gift and realize they are miracles, gifts from the universe, or even our contracts and lessons coming true, we connect to the oneness of the universal spirit, our hearts fly open and we feel the love from within our own selves. The walls that we built around us, our fortresses of distrust, anger, hurt, bitterness and resentment melt away when loving gratitude steps forth. Look at the gifts Michele, Judy and Susan experienced. You can feel the gratitude from these people, gratitude for all those lessons and self growth.

> *Lori's situation: Step 4.* I feel blessed beyond words to have had those experiences, and I can tell you, of course, there have been many, many other blessings that I have received through forgiveness. I can honestly say that I would not change one single thing that has happened to me. I found a strength I did not know I had. I am totally grateful for the life my new husband and I have created. And I am proud that I was able to support and raise my children on my own. I am blessed. And it is from the place, of feeling forgiveness, gratitude and peace in my own past, from which I am able to feel and create love in my current life.

**A Meditation for You,
Living with Forgiveness:**

Take a deep breath please, right now, and remember a time when someone hurt you. Acknowledge and accept what they did. Now, take another breath, what did you do or feel that contributed in someway to that hurtful incident? Take the time to see your part in the story. Now, what did you learn from the experience? How did it change who you are? Take a moment and acknowledge all the gifts. Take another deep breath in and let your shoulders drop with the out breath. FEEL love and gratitude in your heart for the gift you gained in this lifetime. See how something that someone did for you, how they played a role for you to grow and heal, changed you forever. See that person in front of you and say and FEEL “Thank YOU!” Take another deep breath, place your hands on your heart, feel thank you again. This is gratitude. This is what Forgiveness feels like. This is Living Forgiveness.

~~~*~*~~~
~~~

Chapter 6

Forgiving the Unforgivable

"In a way, forgiving is only for the brave. It is for those people who are willing to confront their pain, accept themselves as permanently changed, and make difficult choices. Countless individuals are satisfied to go on resenting and hating people who wrong them. They stew in their own inner poisons and even contaminate those around them. Forgivers, on the other hand, are not content to be stuck in a quagmire. They reject the possibility that the rest of their lives will be determined by the unjust and injurious acts of another person."

~ Beverly Flanigan
Author of *Forgiving The Unforgivable: Overcoming the Legacy of Intimate Wounds*
(Wiley, 1994)

I notice that "unforgivable" has a different connotation depending on your perspective. What one person finds "unforgivable" another has no problem forgiving. The powerful heartfelt stories in this chapter need little comment. They speak for themselves. Please hold the writers in light and love as you read and receive the gifts they share with you: especially the gift of "If I can do it, so can you!"

This chapter is difficult for me to write, because I am now of the belief that NOTHING is "unforgivable." I ask for guidance on how in the world to explain the importance of forgiving something that is, in our human minds, abhorrent. These "unforgivables" are the violations of all our rules, our fundamental and core beliefs. These "unforgivables" get in the way of us feeling safe and secure in the world. They challenge our ability to breathe, get up in the morning, smile, eat, and to function in the world at large. When someone experiences these "unforgivables," their life will never be the same again!

We are in truth spirit having a human experience whose purpose is to learn the lessons we have not yet mastered in prior human lifetimes. We agreed to come to earth forgetting who we really are so we can fully experience the intricacies of duality. In the spirit world, we remember and we know we are all one and that we are Love. From the vantage point of being on the other side, when we are on earth, we will somehow know that those who love us the most are helping us with our lessons by playing the 'bad guy' for us. If we *remembered*, we would also *remember* that we have love enough inside of us to be the 'bad guy' for our loved one's personal growth in other lifetimes. We would *remember* that we all come from one source, God/Love. In the spirit world, our oneness allows us to be on the same page as the other person. In the spirit world, there is no room to doubt or question another's intention, because we *know* who we really are. This is why we love to come to Earth, we get to play the game of duality and be challenged in a totally different way.

We know that ultimately there is nothing to forgive, because it was a plan we created, a plan that enhances our own personal growth.

There is no anger, regret, or bitterness when we remember.
There is only gratitude and love for a job well done.

To make the plan work, we needed to forget who we really are. We think we are separate from each other. We forget that as one hurts another, one has been hurt too. Our interconnectedness makes this so.

And this is why your thoughts are so powerful. Imagine when you are constantly thinking negative thoughts about yourself or others, you are literally weakening your body – which in turn makes it more susceptible to dis-ease. Mind-body-spirit medicine is not new age; it's just that we in the west are finally recognizing what the east already knew.

How in the world do you heal and forgive the "unforgivable?" My friend, forgiveness expert Brenda Adelman shares her powerful and inspiring story with you, which can shift your mindset about whether or not forgiveness can in fact help you find more peace and happiness in your life.

Forgiving the Unforgivable

In 1995, my father shot and killed my mother. Within a month, he moved in with my aunt, my mother's sister and they married soon after. My life spiraled out of control. All the love I had for my father turned into hate as he refused to answer my questions about the specifics of what happened the night my mother died. The reason he didn't answer was because he was guilty.

The facts told me everything I truly needed to know: his gun, the gun I learned to shoot as a child, the gun he had with him every day, the gun that he stored under his pillow in my parents' bedroom at night (in case of an intruder) vanished during the eight hours after my mother died and before the police were called. It was not my father who informed them of my mother's death, but his attorney, who let them know there was a 'dead body' in the house I grew up in. Nothing more. My father did not talk to the police, ever. His lawyer did the talking.

The excruciating grief and the co-dependence with my father were so severe that I moved automatically into denial. I denied the facts and refused to believe that my father had murdered my mother in cold blood and had thought about it enough in advance to have everything in place that he needed to complete the cover-up.

I denied my rage by shaming myself for it as I tried to continue being 'daddy's little girl.' I spoke with him daily swallowing my rage with small talk about our health concerns and my desire to heal my overly sensitive stomach.

I stopped eating or sleeping regularly, awake only to the obsessive thoughts of my mind. My thoughts vacillated between wishing my father had killed himself after he killed my mother, wishing I could shoot him dead and wanting to put a gun in my mouth and pull the trigger.

Three years later, when I confided in a friend from acting class that I fantasized about killing myself, he said something that changed me forever. He said, "You know Brenda, if you take your life you won't ever be with your mom again."

The thought of that pierced my heart, and something cracked. If I would not be with my mom again then what was the point of wanting to die to rejoin her? I took a breath as tears fell from my eyes. It was time to be present and make my mom proud.

It would take years of unraveling, expressing the darkness I was feeling through my art and in therapy, completing a two year master's degree in spiritual psychology, exploring my Judaism and embracing the principles of the Church of Religious Science and Unity Church to start healing. And most importantly, I had to heal my codependence, to learn how to enforce healthy boundaries with my father before I would truly heal.

Knowing at the core of my being that there is a universal presence that is good and expresses through everyone helped me to recognize the good in my dad, despite his actions that night. Having an insight that if I hated any part of my father I was also hating a part of myself inspired me to forgive any and all judgments of him, which also led me to forgiving the judgments I held against myself and my mother. From this place, I was able to make self-honoring decisions based on love.

One of these decisions was to take my father to court for the wrongful death of my mom. He skipped town with his wife, my aunt, disallowing me from collecting a multi-million dollar judgment. I continued to release the hold my righteousness and sense of right and wrong had on me. I loved myself too much to be steeped in that anger.

From this place of openness and strength I wrote a one-person show based on my life, titled My Brooklyn Hamlet, which I have performed internationally. I started teaching the steps I took to forgive to trainers in the domestic violence field, college students and youth at risk and I have been blessed with the best relationship in my life. As my heart opened so did my world.

Brenda Adelman
www.ForgivenessandFreedom.com

When I read Brenda's story, I always wonder, from a spiritual perspective, what the obviously convoluted plan was and who was to learn what and how each person's soul was to be helped by this situation. How is it that Brenda can forgive something so horrific that our human minds can barely comprehend, while another person can not forgive something seemingly easier, such as adultery? We are all on different levels of soul advancement. In other words, a human who is okay being a thief might not be an advanced soul while another human who steals might be doing it as a favor for someone else's lesson, e.g., to learn boundaries and to stand up for herself, and is a very advanced soul. How do you know what level of soul advancement you are? My guess is that Brenda, in being able to forgive her father this deep violation, is a very advanced soul. No wonder she is touching the lives of many with her one-person play, coaching, and teachings about forgiveness.

Through in-between life regressions, people can often access and see their soul and soul family. They often know how advanced they are as a soul and from that place, they have no ego or judgment about it. If you are interested in understanding your soul's evolution on the physical plane, you can look up the Michael Teachings. Michael is a group of over 1,000 souls that channeled information to help humans understand their soul's life plans. [18]

What is unforgivable? As I said earlier, nothing. Yet, humans need to have experiences that are the impetus for our soul's growth. That is why I am including a number of stories here, true stories, to allow you to really understand what it takes for someone to forgive what we would typically call "unforgivable."

When all else fails, waking up to the understanding that we are all One, allows forgiveness to flow and healing, real healing, to take place.

I want to share an excerpt from Immaculée Ilibagiza's book, Left to Tell: Discovering God Amidst the Rwandan Holocaust (2007, Hay House, Inc., Carlsbad CA). She was a Tutsi refugee hiding in a bathroom with 7 other women for 90 days in a pastor's house. This is one of the most profound experiences of forgiveness I have ever read. Take a deep breath and go into your heart as you read this.

> "Look in that!" One of them yelled. "Now look under here. Move that chest! *Search everything!*"
>
> I covered my mouth with my hands, fearing that they'd hear me breathing. They were only

inches from my head . . . . The floor was creaking in front of the wardrobe – *the wardrobe*! I thanked God again for it, but my heart still thumped against my chest.

I could hear them *laughing*. They were having fun while going about killing people! I cursed them, wishing that they'd burn in hell.

The wardrobe banged against the door. I covered my ears and prayed: *God, please. You put the wardrobe there . . . now keep it there! Don't let them move it. Save us, Lord!*

My scalp was burning, and the ugly whispering slithered in my head again: *Why are you calling on God? Don't you have as much hatred in your heart as the killers do? Aren't you as guilty of hatred as they are? You've wished them dead; in fact, you wished that you could kill them yourself! You even prayed that God would make them suffer and make them burn in hell.*

I could hear the killers on the other side of the door, and entreated, *God, make them go away . . . . Save us from –*

Don't call on God, Immaculée, the voice broke in. He knows that you're a liar. You lie every time you pray to Him to say that you love Him. Didn't God create us all in His image? How can you love God but hate so many of His creations?

Finally, I heard the killers leaving. First they left the bedroom, then the house, and soon they were walking away down the road, their singing fading in the distance.

I resumed my prayers. I thanked God for saving us and for giving me the idea to put the wardrobe in front of the bathroom door. *That was so smart of You, God. You are very smart,* I said mentally, and thanked Him again. I wondered where the killers were off to, then I started praying for my friends and family: *Please look over my mother, God, she worries so much about us. Watch over my father; he can be so stubborn . . . .*

It was no use – my prayers felt hollow. A war had started in my soul, and I could no longer pray to a God of love with a heart full of hatred.

I tried again, praying for Him to forgive the killers, but deep down I couldn't believe that they deserved it at all. It tormented me . . . . I tried to pray for them myself, but I felt like I was praying for the devil. *Please open my heart, Lord, and show me how to forgive. I'm not strong enough to squash my hatred – they've wronged us all so much . . . . My hatred is so heavy that it could crush me. Touch my heart, Lord, and show me how to forgive.*

I struggled with the dilemma for hours on end. I prayed late into the night, all through the next day, and the day after that, and the day after that. I prayed all week, scarcely taking food or water. I couldn't remember when or how long I'd slept, and was only vaguely aware of time passing.

One night I heard screaming not far from the house, and then a baby crying. The killers must have slain the mother and left her infant to die in the road. The child wailed all night; by morning, its cries were feeble and sporadic, and by nightfall, it was silent. I heard dogs snarling nearby and shivered to think how that baby's life had ended. I prayed for God to receive the child's innocent soul, and then asked Him, *How can I forgive people who would do such a thing to an infant?*

I heard His answer as clearly as if we'd been sitting in the same room chatting: *You are all my children . . . and the baby is with Me now.*

It was such a simple sentence, but it was the answer to the prayers I'd been lost in for days.

In God's eyes, the killers were part of His family, deserving of love and forgiveness. I knew that I couldn't ask God to love me if I was unwilling to love His children. At that moment, I prayed for the killers, for their sins to be forgiven. I prayed that God would lead them to recognize the horrific error of their ways before their life on Earth ended – before they were called to account for their mortal sins.

> I held on to my father's rosary and asked God to help me, and again I heard His voice: *Forgive them; they know not what they do.*
>
> I took a crucial step toward forgiving the killers that day. My anger was draining from me – I'd opened my heart to God, and He'd touched it with His infinite love. For the first time, I pitied the killers. I asked God to forgive their sins and turn their souls toward His beautiful Light.
>
> That night I prayed with a clear conscience and a clean heart. For the first time since I entered the bathroom, I slept in peace.

The experience of peace, I believe, also comes from the place of "oneness" that we have all been what we would consider good **and** evil. On some level, when we forgive those who have caused hurt or evil against us, we are, in essence, forgiving ourselves for those past lifetimes where we have also committed hurt or evil against another.

"You are all my children."
~ God

I want to share with you a view from the outside, from the 'other side of the veil' about the importance of forgiveness and the differences between how we on Earth view our lessons versus how they are viewed from the higher spiritual plane.

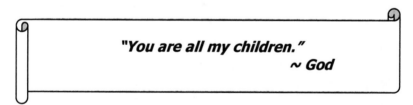

Channeled Akashic Record [19]
Reading on Forgiveness

As I talked to you, ... we ... enter the hall of Akashic records. And there is always a guide, an angel, a truth teller, that enters and I feel I have this whole chorus around us, holding hands.

All is right and here is the message: Forgiving the Unforgiveable .... We don't have that over here, because it isn't – because it's an earth thing, that's the only thing that's coming to me, that these are the agreements that are set before you even cross over. And to one, what may be unforgivable is forgivable to another. These big "unforgivables" are the lessons that make you the person that you become, as hard as they may feel, as sad as you may get. That, as you become more aware and you elevate in your spirit that even though it may seem hard, you know that you put this in your path for the reason that you have in your human life: to teach you, to guide you, to make you a better person.

They're acknowledging that before I sat down I was clearing my head and dropping into my heart because we can get so "heady" and that's where the unforgiveness comes from. It's always the messages that are floating around in our head not what's really in our heart. And as you move from those loud outcries of your head to pay attention to me, because I am so hurt. I am the victim. Poor me. Moving from that and into your heart is the way to ask the questions of yourself. What is the lesson? Why me? And then it's a spiritual, why me? It's not a victim, why me?

I'm just going to shoot up some words that are coming to me – transcendental, shift and change, bigger than – bigger than you can imagine – that one got me choked up – truth and light, and most of all love. Because it's not until you can move into love that you can forgive. Moving out of your head of the unthinkable and into your heart of the imaginable; that's the dream.

Akashic Records
Channeled through Christine Laureano
www.ChristineLaureano.com

Christine's own personal story, of losing her daughter, is heart wrenching, moving, and so inspirational. She has lived the fear of every mother and has come out the other side, as you will see.

Christine's Story:

Hurt, numb, devastated, gone!

When I go back to that day and try to describe it today, these are the four words that come to me. The pain and devastation was too great to bear.

On May 5, 1995 my 4 month 22 day old baby girl, still in her carrier, was placed on a water bed for a nap at an in-home daycare. Checked on only once in 3 hours, she was found overturned, still strapped into her carrier, suffocated. My baby died in daycare. To this day, it is still unknown how this terrible tragedy occurred.

My husband and I arrived at the hospital within moments of each other. We were ushered into a small room adjacent from the emergency room. "We think it was SIDS." the nurse told us. I actually had to say, "You mean my daughter died?" We walked into a parent's worst nightmare.

Over the next couple of weeks, the only way to soothe our aching hearts was to "accept" that SIDS is Divine Intervention. A going home of an Angel.

We started the long walk of healing our broken hearts only to have it broken further. What was first thought as SIDS, 6 weeks later was determined as a case of suffocation. Someone entered the room where our daughter was asleep. She was on a waterbed. She was found overturned, completely face down, strapped in the carrier – suffocated. Now, it was at the hand of someone, not Divine Intervention. It was someone's fault!

Unforgivable?

After knowing the truth I went into hole that I never thought I would get out of. I spent a month on the couch, not moving, crying, sleeping, trying to wake up from this awful dream. Finally, from a still small place, I decided that this was not the kind of mom I wanted to be. There were only two ways I could go; two choices. I could spiral down further or I could spiral up and live my agreement.

I had no idea how I was going to do this. First, I had to get up off the couch and shower. I had to get out of the house. I wasn't ready to see people I knew. I could not tell the story again. I needed people, but I also needed to be alone. I ended up at the bookstore. Books have always helped me learn what's next; business, creativity, enjoyment and now my life.

I wandered through the passages of books, looking for something. I had no idea what. Then a book on Angels caught my eye. I looked and continued wandering. And then, came upon more Angels. It was time to step out of the world and into the Divine. That book on Angels was just what I needed to begin the spiral upward.

That happened 17 years ago. What was first an unforgivable tragedy has become a life lesson in forgiveness.

Forgiveness does not mean what happened is OK.

Forgiveness, for me, means letting go of the energy that is keeping me bound to the hurt. In the many books on Angels and spiritual growth, since the day I turned my life back on, I have learned to ask for what I need and to listen for the message that will help move me in the right direction. The message for forgiveness was that message – loud and clear.

Imagine being in a corral with the person/people that has caused you harm, pain or frustration. You are trapped with this person, to wander through life bound to each other, unless you decide to open the corral gates and let that person out. You release them from your space, from your energy field. It doesn't mean that you condone their behavior; after all, it's theirs to own and work through, not yours.

We have enough to work through in this lifetime. Holding onto someone else's lessons will not help you elevate spiritually, mentally or emotionally.

Forgiveness, letting go and trusting your heart, working through and releasing the pain, is the way to bring your energy home.

Easy? No, it's not easy. It was not easy for me. As a matter of fact, it is the hardest thing I've ever had to do in my life. But I found that on the other side is lightness, self-love and a life that fully opens up. I learned to honor my desires and how to invite people back in with grace.

Christine Laureano
www.ChristineLaureano.com

When Christine was channeling the Akashic Records, I thought I would just ask the records about her losing her child. I said, "[u]sing Christine as an example, in losing her daughter at such a young age, there are few things that humans experience that feel more unforgiveable than that. What was it about Christine that allowed her to forgive and move on? What did she do?"

The Akashic Records, still being channeled through Christine, answered:

> *We love this example. Okay, I'm going to talk as the guides, not me. What Christine went through at first was unimaginable and unforgiving. As Christine went through her lesson, the tough one that it was, let's just say we put a lot of information and opportunities in front of her to grow. She stayed stuck for a really long time even though she had the information to move on and to grow – the spiritual information, all the books, and all the readings. It wasn't until a point where Christine assimilated this information and took it to heart. It's very tearing. It was the moment at which they said good-bye that it changed her understanding and her connection with her daughter and she was open enough to hear the words that this is bigger than you, this is bigger than the accident, and this is bigger than the woman that was involved. This is a life lesson not of the one, but of the many. And as she moved into that we embraced her and we watched her forgive.*
>
> *There's an example she uses all the time which was one of the gifts we gave her. Imagine you're in a corral, a gated corral, with a person that you believe wronged you. Do you want that person to stay stuck with you your entire life in this corral? The misunderstanding is that forgiving is not forgetting. Forgiving is not condoning. Forgiving is very*

> *spiritual. It's allowing the life lesson to pass through you in order to elevate.*
>
> *Forgiveness is like unlocking the corral door and letting that person out, so you no longer have to sit with the pain and the hurt; the forgiveness is the open door. They will work through their life lesson. As long as you work through yours, you will transcend, you will move forward. You will heal and you will change. Wow, that was cool because I saw that from a totally different angle. Thank you for asking that.*

I wanted to include all of these aspects of forgiveness so you could feel and understand the enormity of what is really involved in each of our lessons. You might have a knowing, a belief that it contains one particular lesson, but sometimes the lessons are unknown for years, or the lessons may never be known during this lifetime. Sometimes, the other people involved have additional lessons. As it turned out, many years later, the woman involved in Christine's child's death lost someone close to her too.

And then another tough question arises when something horrible is done to you. What if you were an innocent child who was abused? What if you've had a lifetime of abuse? How do you forgive a person who has a duty to love and protect you, yet instead destroys your emotional and psychological fabric? Author, producer, and inspirational speaker, Sharon Lund has a lot to say about this, and I am pleased to be able to share her story with you:

Sharon's Story:

My childhood innocence was taken away by my grandfather who sexually abused me for nine years. The fear, confusion, anger, hatred, resentment and pain caused me to feel filthy, betrayed, helpless and ashamed. My grandfather's voice echoed throughout every cell of my Being, "If you tell anyone, I will kill your Mommy." I kept silent and prayed to God to be saved and end my suffering.

This silence manifested in repeated sore throats, despair and terrifying nightmares. I had low self-esteem, lack of confidence, deep-seated feelings of depression, and always felt like I never fit in.

My second marriage, to a man named Bill, was equally destructive with more abuse and emotional and mental suffocation. After only six months of marriage, we were divorced. Afterwards, I accidentally discovered that he knowingly infected me with HIV/AIDS. That seemed like the fatal blow.

My abuse and silence around the abuse suffered at the hands of both these men devastated me. My thoughts were consumed with negativity. I became anorexic and attempted suicide, because I thought killing myself was the only way I could end my suffering.

I was hospitalized and while there, my doctor encouraged me to call my parents and tell them about the years of abuse. It was that phone call that turned my life around. It was then that I realized how important it was for me to break my silence, and forgive the men who had caused me so much pain. It was then that I decided that I was no longer a victim.

I realized that as long as I held onto my UNforgiveness of them, that the torment had a hold on my life and my well-being. I didn't deny or try to minimize the hurt. I still felt it, but I no longer allowed the hurt to control me. I took responsibility for my feelings and wrote about them. I prayed for forgiveness, not only for them but also for myself, to find compassion and understanding. Through this forgiveness work, I was able to reclaim my power and dignity. I realized forgiveness was for me and no one else. It was what saved me. Before long, I started to love myself.

Soon, I understood that out of this trauma came courage, and that even through the dark periods of my life I was able to remember the Divinity within me. I realized that these men had brought me into greater alignment with the truth of who I am, and now I can call them "blessings" in my life. Through those experiences, I have now found inner peace, courage, strength, compassion, love, healing and Oneness. My life is filled with lessons that, on some level, I know I agreed to and I have become a better person because of what these lessons have taught me.

I now passionately live my life purpose with dignity and grace because I know that God never gives us more than what we can handle.

Sharon Lund, DD
www.SacredLife.com

The gifts and blessings of Sharon NOT letting these "unforgivables" define and defeat her benefit all of us. She has helped thousands deal with death and dying, teaching and "proving" that we are spirit, not just a human body. What Sharon brings to the table is grace, love, and the ability after not one, but two near-death experiences, to teach people what truly matters and what truly is sacred in our lives. She is here to help us all *remember*.

But it's not fair!!!

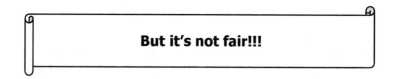

I first started thinking about forgiveness and God and life being so unfair when I was 17, working in the high school library. I read everything I could get my hands on about the Holocaust. I became obsessed trying to figure out with how this could happen. How could people let this happen? How in the world do you forgive such a thing? This was also the year the mini-series, "Holocaust" was on TV. For years I tried to wrap my mind around this event, as well as other genocides in the world. Where was God? Where was God while millions were being brutally tormented, tortured, humiliated and slaughtered?

Holocaust survivor and author of *Man's Search for Meaning* (1969, ed. 2006) Viktor Frankl, teaches us that in even in the most humiliating conditions imaginable, in Nazi Concentration Camps, humans have the choice of how to behave and what to believe. He reminds us that the human being created the gas chambers and the human being walked into them. In our soul's evolution, we certainly could have been both. I know this is oh so hard to imagine. We have been both rich and poor, lived in various cultures, been different colors and religions, and yes, some have been the killers and torturers as well as the murdered. In the camps, some people remembered the sacredness of life and in their minds and in their hearts, *remembered* God, and *remembered* they were eternal.

With permission, I am sharing one of many stories with you from the website, *The Forgiveness Project*, as an example for forgiving the unforgivable.

Eva Kor, an Auschwitz Holocaust Survivor, was a victim at the age of ten, along with her twin sister Miriam Mozes, of Dr. Josef Mengele, who used them for medical experiments. Both survived, but Miriam died in 1993 when she developed cancer of the bladder most likely as a consequence of the experiments done to her as a child. Eva Kor has since spoken explicitly about her experiences at Auschwitz and founded The C.A.N.D.L.E.S. Holocaust Museum in Indiana where she now lives. In 2003 the museum was destroyed in an arson attack, terrorists believed to be white supremacists.

Eva's Story:

Miriam and I were part of a group of children who were alive for one reason only – to be used as human guinea pigs. During our time in Auschwitz we talked very little. Starved for food and human kindness, it took every ounce of strength just to stay alive. Because we were twins, we were used in a variety of experiments. Three times a week we'd be placed naked in a room, for 6–8 hours to be measured and studied. It was unbelievably demeaning.

In another type of experiment they took blood from one arm and gave us injections in the other. After one such injection I became very ill and was taken to the hospital. Dr. Mengele came in the next day, looked at my fever chart and declared that I had only two weeks to live. For two weeks I was between life and death but I refused to die. If I had died, Mengele would have given Miriam a lethal injection in order to do a double autopsy. When I didn't die he carried on experimenting with us and as a result Miriam's kidneys stopped growing. They remained the size of a child's all her life.

On January 27th 1945, four days before my 11th birthday, Auschwitz was liberated by the Soviet army. After 9 months in refugee camps I returned to my village in Romania to find that no one from my family had survived.

Echoes from Auschwitz were a part of my life but I did not speak publicly about my experiences until 1978 after the television series 'The Holocaust' was aired. People would ask me about the experiments but I couldn't remember very much so I wanted to find other twins who were liberated with me. I wrote to newspapers asking them to publish an appeal for other survivors of Mengele to contact me. By 1980 I was sending out 500 letters a year – but still no response. In desperation one day I decided to start an organization in which I would make myself President. People are always impressed if they get a letter from a president, and it worked. Finally I was able to find other twin survivors and exchange memories. It was an immensely healing experience.

In 1993 I was invited to lecture to some doctors in Boston and asked if I could bring a Nazi doctor with me. I thought it was a mad request until I remembered that I'd once been in a documentary which had also featured a Dr. Hans Munch from Auschwitz. I contacted him in Germany and he said he would meet with me for a videotaped interview to take to the conference. In July 1993 I was on my way to meet this Nazi doctor. I was so scared but when I arrived at his home he treated me with the utmost respect. I asked him if he'd seen the gas chambers. He said this was a nightmare he dealt with every day of his life. I was surprised that Nazis had nightmares too and asked him if he would come with me to Auschwitz to sign a document at the ruins of the gas chambers. He said that he would love to do it.

In my desperate effort to find a meaningful "thank you" gift for Dr. Munch I searched the stores, and my heart, for many months. Then the idea of a Forgiveness letter came to my mind. I knew it would a meaningful gift, but it became a gift to myself as well, because I realized I was NOT a hopeless, powerless victim. When I asked a friend to check my spelling, she challenged me to forgive Dr. Mengele too. At first I was adamant that I could never forgive Dr. Mengele but then I realized I had the power now . . .the power to forgive. It was my right to use it. No one could take it away.

On January 27 1995, at the 50th anniversary of the liberation of Auschwitz, I stood by the ruins of the gas chambers with my children – Dr. Alex Kor and Rina Kor – and with Dr. Munch and his children and grandchild. Dr. Munch signed his document about the operation of the gas chambers while I read my document of forgiveness and signed it. As I did that I felt a burden of pain was lifted from me. I was no longer in the grip of pain and hate; I was finally free.

> *The day I forgave the Nazis, privately I forgave my parents whom I hated all my life for not having saved me from Auschwitz. Children expect their parents to protect them, mine couldn't. And then I forgave myself for hating my parents.*
>
> *Forgiveness is really nothing more than an act of self-healing and self-empowerment. I call it a miracle medicine. It is free, it works and has no side effects.*
>
> *I believe with every fiber of my being that every human being has the right to live without the pain of the past. For most people there is a big obstacle to forgiveness because society expects revenge. It seems we need to honor our victims but I always wonder if my dead loved ones would want me to live with pain and anger until the end of my life. Some survivors do not want to let go of the pain. They call me a traitor and accuse me of talking in their name. I have never done this. Forgiveness is as personal as chemotherapy – I do it for myself.*
>
> Eva Kor
> www.candlesholocaustmuseum.org

If you have been holding onto a story you consider "unforgivable," it is my hope that you are having second thoughts. I think you will agree with me that if the authors of these stories are able to forgive, then you can too. Yes, you have suffered. No one denies the pain and suffering of having something horrific happen to you. Yet, whether you believe God does not give you more than you can handle, or you believe that this is a true personal growth moment for you, I invite you to go through the Living with Forgiveness Process yourself and allow yourself to 'forgive the unforgivable'.

~~~***~~~
~~~

Living with Forgiveness Process

Step 1. Acknowledgment and Acceptance:

Living forgiveness means knowing that we are human and we have strong emotional responses when we feel hurt, unloved, unappreciated and disrespected. It is normal to respond defensively. Acknowledging the truth, "I am devastated. It feels like you really 'f – ked' me over! How am I ever going to recover from this one? You've destroyed any chance of happiness I ever had!" I cannot emphasize enough how important it is to honor your feelings about the situation you need to forgive. Do not allow the seeds of hurt, resentment, bitterness or anger to grow inside you. Speak your truth. Feel your truth. Acknowledge and accept your truth.

The stories in this chapter are just a few examples of what some might call the unforgivable. However, these people know that to have a happy life, they MUST forgive. Would anyone blame Brenda for being angry the rest of her life? No. Would Brenda choose to live the rest of her life in anger, NO! That is the difference.

No one would deny Christine's right to be angry for the rest of her life, would they? No one would deny Sharon's right to put up walls and not let anyone in, would they?

Of course they went through the time they needed to FEEL all those feelings and emotions, seeing their worlds turned upside down. Imagine how Christine felt when she saw her beautiful little baby girl was no longer alive! Imagine Brenda getting the call that her mother was murdered, and then finding out it was her father who killed her! Imagine Sharon watching TV and finding out her husband infected her with HIV! There are no words to describe what this must have been like.

Acknowledgment and acceptance are huge words in this case. Accept means to face the reality of the situation, not to condone it. It means to accept that this did in fact happen and yes, your life is in fact changed forever. That is the reality. Your life is changed forever. It is only from facing this reality that you can start living again. Some people will try to avoid the reality and some will try to ignore the feelings that come up. At some point to live a healthy life, it is necessary to make a choice to ACCEPT what has happened and move forward. The pain is real.

Imagine the pain, the devastation and humiliation that both Immaculée and Eva felt.

So, FEEL those FEELINGS. Really wallow in the muck of hurt and devastation for a period of time. Then take a deep breath and make the choice, the choice to LIVE AGAIN. The choice is to not be defined for the rest of your life by the lowest point in your life, but to live somehow, knowing your life will never be the same again. The sacredness of LIFE is awaiting you. Once this choice is made, you will actually smile again. You might even find love again. You will laugh again and you will even feel happiness again.

Step 2. Personal Responsibility:

Taking personal responsibility might be a difficult lesson to swallow because it does not seem to fit into those situations where something happens to you from the outside, something you seemingly had nothing to do with; however, this is where the leap of faith comes that YOU ARE A SPIRITUAL BEING HAVING A HUMAN EXPERIENCE, AND THIS WAS ALL PART OF THE PLAN! [20]

I know, it makes zero sense to you right now that you would choose to live a life where your child dies, where you get raped, where your daughter chooses an abuser to marry, or where you, as a child, are molested for years on end. It makes no sense at all.

However, think of it this way: If we live many lifetimes to eventually become enlightened, then we need to have experienced of all pieces of this puzzle we call life. We may have lived at least one lifetime as the murderer, the abuser, the abused, the hermit, the monk, the royalty, or the beggar. We have starved, thrived in wealth, cheated, and committed adultery. We had children who died young and we died young as children. We were crippled and we were addicts. If you are reading this book, it is likely you are an advanced soul and have had many lifetimes. When you think about all the possibilities of people out there in the world, know that in some of your other lifetimes, you too were those people, having those experiences and those lessons.

In the regression work I do, many people recognize when they see why they chose the people they reincarnated with in this lifetime. They see the gifts (see next step) and understand that they did in fact choose this person and that person/soul is a close loving soul-mate who incarnated with them to do something we consider awful to them for their soul's growth. Think about this. If your soul chooses to work on the lessons surrounding abuse, would you rather be the abuser or the one being abused? How much does someone have to love you to come here to Earth and be the 'abuser' for your growth?

If you do believe in God, but not in reincarnation, can you step into the place of knowing that God does not give you more than you can handle? God has faith that you can deal with what life has offered you, and that you can have a meaningful life in spite of the fact that terrible things have happened to you. I ask you to step into this alternative view and accept that God loves you and knows you will be okay, and the Spirit who is You is already more than okay.

For those of you who do not believe in God, or reincarnation, what does taking personal responsibility look like for you? Is life all an accident or do you create your own future? Are you in charge? Do you believe in fate? Is there any pre-destination?

Either way, please know that taking personal responsibility for your life is one of the most important choices you can make. If you are unhappy, hurt, or bitter due to something awful that has happened to you, you need to take personal responsibility for how you respond to that situation. Do you want to remain miserable the rest of your life? Do you choose to drink, take drugs, eat too much, act out sexually, waste your money, or just be grouchy and mean to everyone around you because something "unforgivable" happened to you? I don't think so. Suck it up, take a deep breath, and make a choice to live the best, most positive life you can possibly live given your circumstances!

Step 3. Finding the Gift:

There is a gift in every situation. For Brenda she learned how to set healthy boundaries with her father, how to stick up for herself, and learned that staying angry at her father and aunt was only hurting herself. She became a forgiveness teacher and brings her gifts as an actor to others in her one person show, "My Brooklyn Hamlet."

Christine found a spiritual path that has led her to open her heart and trust herself, and to be clear about what lessons are hers and what lessons belong to others. She shares her gifts with others, helping people gain clarity and "live life on purpose!"

Sharon learned that her lessons, as tough as they were, brought her into alignment with who she is at her core, a courageous woman at one with all and a Spirit having a human experience. She lives her life with dignity and the grace of God, teaching others the same.

Immaculée learned that we are all God's children, and that our own hatred, even when directed towards someone whose behavior is abhorrent by all societal standards, is still un-Godly. It is only through our love that we find peace.

Eva found that peace when she let go of 50 years worth of hatred and being controlled by the tormenting memories of her childhood. Teaching others that the power of forgiveness released her from remaining a victim, she is now the victor over her life!

Step 4. Gratitude:

Every single person in this section has said that they found blessings in the aftermath of the horror they experienced. How does the human spirit survive and thrive after the "unforgivable?" Are these unusually strong, brave, or courageous people? Now they are, AFTER finding forgiveness. It is in the experience of forgiveness that they found strength, compassion, spiritual connection, understanding, joy, and divine spiritual love. You too have in you what it takes to forgive. Live every day in gratitude, noticing and focusing your attention on what is good and what is right with your world. No matter what happens, when you "forgive the unforgivable" and release those grudges, anger, hurt, devastation, guilt, shame, bitterness, you will experience lightness and a spiritual cleansing. For that, you can be grateful every day of your life.

I want to share these quotes with you from Anne Frank,[21] they are a good reminder of what your thoughts can be even when you are facing your deepest, darkest days.

> *"It's really a wonder that I haven't dropped all my ideals, because they seem so absurd and impossible to carry out. Yet I keep them, because in spite of everything, I still believe that people are really good at heart."*

> *"Human greatness does not lie in wealth or power, but in character and goodness. People are just people, and all people have faults and short-comings, but all of us are born with a basic goodness."*

~~~***~~~
~~~

Chapter 7

Self Empowerment

Forgiving Ourselves and Forging Ahead Beyond Guilt and Shame

> *"I don't know if I continue even today, always liking myself. But what I learned to do many years ago was to forgive myself. It is very important for every human being to forgive herself or himself because if you live, you will make mistakes – it is inevitable. But once you do and you see the mistake, then you forgive yourself and say, 'well, if I'd known better I'd have done better,' that's all. So you say to people who you think you may have injured, 'I'm sorry,' and then you say to yourself, 'I'm sorry.' If we all hold on to the mistake, we can't see our own glory in the mirror because we have the mistake between our faces and the mirror; we can't see what we're capable of being. You can ask forgiveness of others, but in the end the real forgiveness is in one's own self. I think that young men and women are so caught by the way they see themselves. Now mind you. When a larger society sees them as unattractive, as threats, as too black or too white or too poor or too fat or too thin or too sexual or too asexual, that's rough. But you can overcome that. The real difficulty is to overcome how you think about yourself. If we don't have that we never grow, we never learn, and sure as hell we should never teach."*
>
> ~ Maya Angelou

What we want most in life is to love and be loved. But it is hard to love and be loved when we lack wholeness and do not love ourselves. When what we want is love, but try to force it through a shattered self-image, we end up attracting others who can only love us back to the extent that we ourselves are able to love! Unfortunately, when that happens, we end up with someone mirroring back to us our lack of love or wholeness and we are disappointed. We gather up the broken pieces and off we go again, seeking something or someone else outside ourselves to make us whole, and the cycle repeats.

Our ability to love ourselves is directly related to the thoughts we think.

One of the most powerful self-love lessons we humans can learn is to master our thoughts and therefore our emotions. Our entire day, our week, and our lifetime is manipulated and designed by our thoughts. Think about this: NOTHING is ever created without first being a thought. This is why having self-discipline over our thoughts is perhaps the greatest instrument of transformation of all time.

This is why I am madly in love with the concept of forgiveness. We can move from hurt, through anger, leap over bitterness, and knock over resentment to find ourselves in a place of peace and tranquility. Ultimately, all this transformation is simply choosing to see things differently.

No forgiveness discussion would be complete without talking about self-forgiveness. There are times in everyone's life where we are embarrassed or ashamed by our own behavior and judgments. Some of us can forgive, and let ourselves off the hook. Others of us will punish ourselves forever. We wallow in shame and guilt and never let ourselves off the hook. People involved in 12 step programs know this litany well. They must take an inventory of their past wrongs and try to apologize or repair the harm they have caused. This is a beautiful, yet painful process.

Negative self-talk creates self-hatred. It is abusive. Not believing we are good enough **just as we are** might have begun with an incident, or a pattern in childhood, but it continues and is permeated by our own negative self-talk. Where does this negative self talk come from? Well, only you can answer this question for yourself. You can go back and examine your own inner-child issues, or you can just decide you are sick and tired of remaining a prisoner of your own negative, disempowering thoughts and do the work of letting go and accepting. Allow your inner guidance to teach you. If you are stuck in finding the "right way" to forgive yourself, then the number one thing you can do for yourself is to give up the belief that there is a right or wrong way.

Does God love only the good in us or the good among us? NO. God loves all of us. Yet, we spend a great deal of time trying to do the right thing, be the "good one" or the "right one," hoping to somehow win favor with God, or with our own vision of ourselves. God loves us exactly as we are . . . the good and the shadow (not so good) side. When you blame and criticize others, you are avoiding a truth about yourself. What is the truth you are trying to avoid? Let's just deal with it and get it out of the way!

Personally, I feel like I have wasted way too much time in my life concentrating on what is wrong with me, rather than what is right with me. I found my journal from when I was 11 years old. In it I was complaining about how fat I was. For 40 years, that has been a focus point of my life – my weight! Do you think maybe I could have spent my time in more useful endeavors? Obviously, this became an obsession that I needed to end. Forgiving me helped, but first I needed to develop self-love by being more compassionate with myself. I had to end the self-abusive behavior of "shoulding" myself. You might be able to relate to that too.

Truly, it is a choice – a choice to release the negative thinking.

RELEASE SHOULDS.

LET GO OF NEGATIVE SELF-TALK.

STOP WISHING YOU WERE DIFFERENT OR YOUR PAST WAS DIFFERENT.

RELEASE THE OBSESSION WITH THE IDEA THAT YOU ARE A MISTAKE, THAT YOU SHOULD BE SOMETHING YOU ARE NOT.

GOD does not make mistakes.
God's spirit is inside of you.
You cannot be a mistake.
You are a beautiful child of God.
Be the light you were meant to be.

I think that this obsession just became "who I was." It was like it was attached to me, like my skin. Dr. Joe

Dispenza, in his newest book, *Breaking the Habit of Being Yourself: How to Lose Your Mind and Create a New One* (Hay House 2012), explains that the body literally gets stuck in a re-patterning situation based on past actions, and past thoughts and behaviors that get memorized by the body. He says that one way to get out of the pattern is to get your body to believe that your thoughts and behaviors have changed, and that you can do this through meditating and acting as if you are already living the new life you choose to live. In deep meditation, you change your brain waves so that you move from beta into an alpha or theta state (where your subconscious resides) and from there, there is less resistance, and change happens. This is why you hear people say, "meditate, meditate, meditate" if you want to be happy. Dr. Dispenza says our body is the greatest mind-reader we have.

Meditation expert Sarah McLean[22] agrees with Dispenza's views on meditation, and says in addition to "improving focus and contentment, researchers have recently proved that meditation can also foster compassion . . . . Self-compassion reduces feelings of being threatened, insecure and defensive . . . and helps us feel safer and more secure." The goal of course when we want to stop beating ourselves up or obsessing about the past is to bring more acceptance and self-compassion to light within ourselves.

Guilt and Shame

If you are just enmeshed in guilt and shame, and really struggling in this area, here is a little primer on guilt and shame that helped me – and I think you might find it beneficial.

Shame and guilt are ugly mates. If you are holding onto these unattractive partners, I encourage you to release them immediately. They do not make wrongs right. They do not serve anyone and they destroy your health. If you wish to make amends, be healthy, and make a positive contribution to the world from this day forward. Learn from the past. The changes you make will have long-term ramifications on your karma, your health and the world at large.[23]

In a world where there is an abundance of self-help books and study groups, and where ten percent of the US population (that is one out of every ten people!) is on some kind of anti-depressant/anti-anxiety medication to feel happier in their lives; what is it that gets in our way of becoming the healthier, happier people we were meant to be? Why do ten percent of us turn to drugs to aid us in making that happen? What is holding us back from just being healthy and happy?

What you feed your mind,
likewise feeds your body!

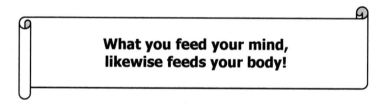

What happens when we fill ourselves with guilt and shame? Our bodies get stuck in a cycle of self-hatred and self-blame. It's easy to get mad at someone who abuses us, but what about when we abuse ourselves? As I said earlier, I was my own worst enemy. I beat myself up worse than anyone else. I was always too fat and not smart enough. In other words, after years of negative self talk, I believed something was inherently wrong with me.

I have always used "guilt and shame" interchangeably or as a grouping, like they are one and the same. I decided I needed to really study the subject and I'd like to share with you what I learned. Let's talk a little about Guilt and Shame.

Definitions Please:

Guilt is based on the past, what we did or didn't do. Guilt was initially taught to us by others, as a way to manipulate our behavior. As children, we wanted to please the adults, and learned that when we violated their rules or moral codes, we were "not good enough."

Author John Bradshaw says the positive aspect of Guilt is that it is "the guardian of our conscious." This helps us as a society live by some kind of moral fabric. We are basically self-regulated by guilt. When we are healthy, we learn from our mistakes and re-calibrate to do better next time.

Shame is another story. Shame is internalizing "I am not good enough," as a core belief.[24] Where guilt is based on an action or inaction, shame is based on what you believe is internally wrong with you. Author John Bradshaw[25] says shame is "the all-pervasive sense that I am flawed and defective as a human being."

Whether taught as a child or something you learned as an adult, there are other core beliefs, like "I am humiliated, embarrassed, worthless or not okay." These feelings are prevalent among addicts and abuse and neglect victims, they often feel more than guilt; they feel shame. Once stuck in the rut of shame, it's hard to forgive yourself because you may feel internally flawed and actually feel a sense of self-loathing. It is like your skin, you just cannot remove it.

Perfect in our imperfections, guilt and shame have become a part of life. Mastering our thoughts and emotions helps us to move through guilt and shame. I have learned something interesting when working with people on forgiveness. People who feel guilt can forgive themselves much easier than people who feel shame. If there is a lot of shame, and you believe something is internally wrong with you, then counseling is really helpful before leaping into forgiveness.

> *"Guilt says 'I have made a mistake,' shame says 'I am a mistake'."*
>
> *~ H. Norman Wright, Grief Psychologist*

If you have an issue with guilt, it's helpful to deal with your "should haves . . . ." I would like you to take some time and do this assignment. First make a list of all your "should haves."

Here is an example: I should have been able to lose weight. I should have called my mother when she was sick. I should have finished college. I should not have had alcohol and drove. I should not have told my daughter she is an idiot. I should have supported my husband more.

Now, change all your "shoulds" into "coulds." Because that is actually truer, it was a choice.

I could have been able to lose weight. I could have called my mother when she was sick. I could have finished college. I could have not had alcohol and drove. I could have not told my daughter she is an idiot. I could have supported my husband more.

Can you feel the difference in the energy between the two paragraphs? The BEATING UP on yourself has been diminished greatly by not "shoulding" yourself. It was a choice. Maybe today with the knowledge you now have you would have chosen differently. That's ok, let it go, we all have things we wish we did differently in the past.

There is a logical process to deal with guilt. This is part of the process in forgiving yourself.

1. Accept and admit what you did. Take responsibility.

2. Apologize by explaining what you did, why you did it, how you understand others were affected by it, and that you are sorry for how it affected the others.

3. Repair the harm if possible.

4. Promise to change that behavior and not do it again.

5. Make the changes you need to make and then daily practice gratitude for the ability to forgive your past!

That's the way it works when you have hurt yourself or others. YOU need a source of love and acceptance. I highly recommend that you do an inner child meditation, (see chapter 10) where you become the unconditional loving parent sending your hurt child the love she/he deserves. You might also choose to turn to God or other spiritual/enlightened beings for that beautiful unconditional love.

My friend Mary has a story to share with you, a story about moving from self-hatred to self-love. Many of us, at least sometime in our lives, have felt these feelings of being different or 'not good enough'.

> *"Forgiveness is a gift you give yourself." I love this and it is so true!*
>
> *At a young age, I felt like I was different. I was always overweight as a child. I was mean, and angry. I was told I was a "bad student" from all my teachers. So I lived up to that title and it became my core belief. I was no good because I wasn't like everyone else. And as I got older, each year I became more filled with hatred towards myself.*
>
> *Because I believed I was not good enough, I did not let myself experience what others were experiencing. For example, I deprived myself of*

having intimate relationships with men and I declined many wonderful job opportunities and of course, never allowed myself to pursue a degree. I isolated myself from the world because of the fear of being rejected. I missed opportunities to be close to relatives and friends. I would not let myself thrive; and I would not let the world see the true Mary.

At one point, I became so numb, mentally, and emotionally. I remember the night that I decided to make a change. I was sitting in my room on the floor and was crying, I cried all night. I have never felt such emptiness and loneliness before, and I became so desperate that I gave myself two choices: 1. Take my life or 2. Change my life. When I started thinking about taking my life, it scared me. That was the motivation I needed to create change. I can't believe how close I came to taking my life.

To change, I realized I just could not carry around the anger and hatred I had towards myself anymore. So I sat down, and just starting writing everything that I was angry at myself for doing, all the mistakes I made, everything. My heart was pouring out and everything I felt just came out onto paper. After an hour of writing I stopped and starting reading over what I had written. I realized I held myself back from living life.

My life became a prison and I was the prisoner and only I had the key to release myself. I did this by slowly visiting the painful places, people and things that brought up so much emotion. I had to feel it and sit with it, until I wasn't angry anymore. It's been a year and a half, still working on it, but so much happier. I realized that I did the best that I could with what I knew at the time, just by saying this has brought me inner peace and strength that I never had before.

I forgave myself for not seeing the beauty of life, only the misery and darkness. Now, I can honestly say that although there are times of struggle, there are many, many more times of peace. I see the beauty all around me. I feel gratitude that I am able to be out there helping others. I am going back to school and pursuing a career. Being able to forgive myself and open the self-imposed prison doors is one of the hardest, yet most rewarding things I've ever accomplished.

Mary Costanza
Salt Lake City, Utah
www.facebook.com/marykcostanza

You can see that what Mary felt was something called "shame." She felt like she was somehow internally flawed. With shame, the illusion of "not good enough" follows you from the past, into the present and the future. Delineation is difficult without professional help. Overcoming shame is about building self-esteem. It is a process. As she said, it is not easy and it is something she still has to work on. If you follow her facebook page, you will see that reaching out to help others who feel the way she felt helps her to stay on the path and build her own self-esteem. Anyone can do this.

Boundaries and Building Self-esteem

Self acceptance is key in building self-esteem. It's about taking responsibility for how you feel about yourself. Sure, you might have been abused your entire childhood, but if you spend all your time in blame, you remain a victim. You have to take personal responsibility for your own happiness. No one else can or will do this for you.

You are your own prisoner.
Use your key and set yourself free!

It is imperative to give up the illusion of being a victim today based on something that happened in the past. You need to make a decision that the pity party stops right now! The past no longer exists but in your own mind. There are millions of people who have been abused or neglected in their childhood, who have been raped, who have family members who have been murdered, who live in pain every single day. Ask yourself, why do some people move on with their lives and find peace while others do not? They have learned that if they keep blaming someone else for their lives, they remain a victim to the very person they are blaming. And worse, if they keep blaming themselves, the guilt and shame will keep them imprisoned forever. The guard who holds the key is YOU.

The people who were able to forgive in these awful scenarios are not special people with extrasensory powers. What they did is simply this: They made a choice to find peace by taking control over their own thoughts! Seriously, it is as simple as that! A choice. Your choice.

> *"Every 60 seconds you spend angry, upset or mad is a full minute of happiness you will never get back."*
>
> *~ Author unknown*

Boundaries are vital in self-esteem. Learning how to set boundaries is all about believing that you deserve respect. If you don't believe it though, then pretend you do and as uncomfortable as it is, demand respect anyway.

Usually when we talk about boundaries, we talk about people walking all over us, (see chapter 9 for more on boundaries with others). For me it was more about me not trusting myself and looking outside of myself for the answers. I know as a healer and teacher, I am very empathic and have had to learn what energy is mine and what energy belongs to others. I had to learn to trust myself. This took practice. I learned that my intuition, my emotional guidance system, is the best tool I have. I also learned that saying "no" was about me listening to myself and giving myself what I needed to remain healthy and whole. Believing that you are worthy and are, in fact, good enough, might start with the most powerful word in the English language: "NO."

I learned that listening to your gut feelings can raise your self esteem. When we practice this regularly, we can discover the truth, that God/spirit/oneness (whatever YOU call it) is alive and well inside every one of us.

I need to have a conversation here with women about being "self-ish." You must learn how to take care of yourself first. This is not selfish, it is being OF SELF. Your wishes and desires are important. You must take personal responsibility for getting your wishes and desires met. In this way, you will have more energy to give to others. Whether it is setting energetic boundaries by not allowing others to suck your energy dry, saying NO to something you do not want to do, or asking for help, creating boundaries to protect yourself is one of the best things you can do to build your self esteem, and eventually, release any shame that you are holding onto.

Self-empowerment also comes from setting strong boundaries, and having clarity in who you are, what your needs are, and how to get them met. Holding onto grudges, self-loathing, and negative self talk destroys the ability to grow spiritually and personally.

This is why we must forgive. If we can forgive ourselves for our perceived wrong doings or lack of worthiness, then forgiving others is a breeze!

I have some questions for you. Do you believe that you deserve to be happy? Do you know who you really are? Do you live life according to YOUR values rather than according to others' values? How harshly do you treat yourself? Can you be kinder, gentler to yourself? Can you give yourself a break? Can you quiet your mind so you stop beating up on you?

I want to share a conversation I had with The Light Beings, as channeled by Dr. Earl Backman, which explains the need for us to forgive ourselves.

> *Earl: In some cases you need to forgive yourself. And you know there are many cases where many individuals cannot forgive themselves. The impact of not forgiving yourself is so detrimental to your soul's progress for it paralyzes you. It shuts you off from being able to love others.*
>
> *Because you can't love yourself if you cannot forgive yourself. And if you cannot love yourself, you cannot love someone else. So you become isolated. And you live in anger and fear, and cut off from your guides and teachers and spirit. This is so important to realize, that forgiving yourself is just as important as forgiving others. Thank you.*

LORI: Thank you. Yeah, I always felt that that was the hardest thing for us to do to forgive our own self.

EARL: It is and it's too difficult for many earth beings to forgive themselves. Because remember, if you can, to forgive yourself for your actions. It is in fact easier for you to forgive others. Because in forgiving yourself, you admit your humanness. You admit you're not perfect. You admit you make mistakes. You admit you do things that cause pain, including pain to yourself. So if you can forgive yourself, then you open the way up to being less judgmental. If you are less judgmental, then you are more forgiving. If you are highly judgmental, then you cannot forgive. That is why we focus so much, and you heard us say this, on love, hope, compassion, acceptances, and understanding. Acceptance and understanding are the keys to forgiveness – for yourself, and forgiveness of others.

Thank you.

Light Beings
Channeled through Dr. Earl Backman
www.ravenheartcenter.com

What would it be like to stop judging yourself? How can you stop judging yourself? Have you ever noticed that when you feel really good about yourself you are actually less judgmental of others? Are you looking for other people to forgive you so you can let yourself off the hook? If you are more understanding and accepting, and stop condemning your own actions, you no longer condemn others. If you were to truly realize that all situations in your life are to teach you to be more accepting of yourself and others, you would understand there is no need for judgment, condemnation, hatred or any other form of fear.

I want to share a couple stories with you of self-forgiveness, where you can see the transformation from self-condemnation to self acceptance, understanding and forgiveness.

The first is from my friend June, who has been in recovery for over 20 years and has helped hundreds of people with her inspirational stories, her love of life and her huge heart. She is a shining example of what happens when you choose to stop beating yourself up for the past, take personal responsibility for what you did, and then choose to make the changes you want to make in your own life.

June's Story:

I believe I have made the best choices I could in my life. I am a 51-year-old woman in recovery. When I got clean and sober, I never thought I would be able to forgive myself for what I put my parents through.

I was adopted. I grew up in New York as an only child with two parents who loved me. I believe that they did the best parenting they could in the way they thought was right. For years my parents experienced terror, confusion and heartache, lessening to disgust and disappointment and eventually, detachment, in response to my actions.

One of the first things my mother said to my birth mother when they met for the first time, was "if I knew where you were, when she was 13, I would have given her back!"

The first time I ran away from home I was 14 years old. I was naïve and hurt. At home I felt misunderstood and criticized. I met some people who seemed to accept me for who I was. I was with them for 3 days and they made arrangements for me to go to South Carolina the next day. On that third day, a detective found me and took me home. Many years later, I realized how lucky I was that the detective found me. Today I believe I was almost sold into prostitution.

When I was in 9th grade, I broke my leg in a motorcycle accident. At the time of the accident, they wanted to amputate below the right knee. That same year I got pregnant and miscarried following one of the surgeries on my leg. My leg was broken for 4 years until it was finally healed with electrical stimulation.

The second time I ran away from home, I was 16 years old and still with a broken leg. Again, I thought I found people who accepted me for who I was, which was not how I felt at home. During the 14 days I was gone, I was drugged so deeply I don't remember much of what happened to me. When the detectives found me this time, I was hiding in the attic. I weighed less than 100 pounds, barely clothed and was so weak I couldn't put up a fight. My parents were standing at the car when they brought me out of the house. They wrapped me in a blanket and took me home. No words were spoken.

When I was 17, I accidently overdosed on seconal, a barbiturate. I called 911 on my self as I thought I was going to die. Charcoal was administered and I am here to tell the story.

When I was 18 years old, I left my parents' home and moved in with my alcoholic boyfriend, age 26. I still had a broken leg. For the next many years my journey was filled with drugs and alcohol, grand adventures and misadventures.

I got clean and sober at age 29 and learned that I could make amends to my parents for what I put them through. I could never give them back the hours of worry, despair and disappointment, but I could make a living amends to them for my past behaviors. I felt incredibly guilty for what I put my parents through.

I watched how other people rebuilt relationships with their parents. For example, I picked Sundays at 11:00 to call my parents each week. In the past, months would go by when my parents would have no contact from me, they had no idea where I was, or if I was still alive.

After my father passed away, I flew regularly from Oregon to California to be of support to my mother. My relationship with her grew and it was the first time since I was a child that we spent time together. We even went on a trip together. When her health started to fail, I spent weeks by her side arranging everything. I was able to be there for her at the end.

Even though my parents said they forgave me for what I put them through, I never thought I would ever forgive myself.

It wasn't until they were both dead that the burden of guilt lifted and the seeds of forgiveness blossomed.

Today I live my life in gratitude, acceptance and forgiveness, less judgment and much more compassion for everyone and especially myself.

Written in honor of the memory of
my mother and father.

One of the most grateful people you will ever meet,

June Sedarbaum
Eugene, Oregon USA

Energetic Forgiveness Visualization

Because so many people are inflicted with an addiction or have hurt someone else, I feel it's important to address this head on. If you are beating yourself up for hurting someone in the past, I want you to do this little exercise: Imagine the person you hurt. Now, take a deep breath and go to your heart space. Take deep breaths until you are there, in your heart. Please picture that person again, the one who you have hurt and bring him/her up in front of you. Now, please look in their eyes and tell them you are sorry and ask for forgiveness. See them lovingly and gratefully accepting that apology. Now, feel how that feels, take it all in. Notice what happens in your body. Even if someone doesn't forgive you in real life, they can forgive you on an energetic level. By releasing them from you needing their forgiveness, energetically you help them too. Remember, we are all one. The gift of forgiveness is out there. Allow it in. Allow it to flow in to you and out from you. I have seen so many miracles happen with this process. If you are willing to stop beating yourself up, you can allow space for a miracle to happen. Are you willing to feel peace? Are you willing to give AND receive the gift of forgiveness? Give it to yourself.

Forgiveness is a gift to give, as well as a gift to receive!

Forgiveness is FOR GIVING to someone else as well as to yourself.

When someone FORGIVES you, they give it for you.

It is your job to receive their gift.

Sometimes it is hard to think of oneself as someone who might have caused someone else pain. It is easier to forget. It is easier to ignore it. Sometimes it is so painful to think we hurt someone else that we literally make excuses for why we did what we did and blame the other person for it. Some of us have become master manipulators to avoid the feelings associated with guilt and shame. Some of us feel anger or rage so explosively that we can not see our role in the situation or the pain we cause.

The truth is, we have all hurt someone else. And, we do not like to think of ourselves as hurting someone else. Earlier in the book, I mentioned my husband broke up with me twice before we were married.

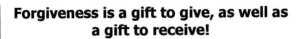

When I bring this up, I know he feels bad because of how it hurt me. His response is usually, "let's not think about that!" I believe that when you love someone and hurt them, it hurts you to know you hurt them. It is easier to "stuff" than it is to accept it.

Like Mary's story above, Robby LeBlanc had a really tough childhood and it went right to his core. The only way he could sooth himself was to eat. It was an addictive behavior. Robby's story was particularly inspirational to me because I could relate to it so well. I hated myself because I was overweight. It was always a struggle for me. Robby had to work to face and overcome severe childhood abuse. He did the arduous work of releasing the "victim" mentality. Now, Robby is inspiring many and just successfully completed a goal he was never really sure he would be able to – he climbed Mt. Kilimanjaro!

Robby's Story:

May 25, 2010 I stepped on the scale and it hit 360 pounds! If I was 7 ft 9 inches tall that may be ok, but I was a mere 5 ft 6 inches! I wasn't obese, I was MORBIDLY obese.

In June of 2010 I was performing a concert at the Red Rock Hotel Casino and in the middle of the concert, as I was playing a guitar solo I realized both my legs and feet were numb. I could not feel them. A few days later I found out the numbness in my legs and feet was from diabetic neuropathy.

July 10, 2010 I received a phone call from a friend of mine and he ask; "Robby, would you be willing to share your story and challenges with your weight and health on film, in exchange for going to a World Class Eating Disorder Clinic? In that moment I realized I was broken. I needed help. This would be filmed for the Oprah Winfrey Network. It was a show called "Addicted To Food."

Exactly 1 month later, from August 10, 2010 for the next 42 days I was at Shades of Hope Eating Disorder Clinic in Buffalo Gap Texas.

This was INTENSE Rehab. No TV, radio, internet, newspapers, magazines, or cell phone for the next 42 days. They also took away my guitar. They made me FACE my issues. I had never cried so much in my entire life! This was the first time I had confronted a number of issue's that had really been bothering me and I wasn't even consciously aware of it.

Prior to going to Shades of Hope, I had lost all hope and confidence in myself and abilities. I was a victim. I blamed everything and everybody for why my life, my finances, my music, my health was not working out the way I had dreamed.

Attending Shades made me very aware of my choices and actions. Some people have a problem with drugs, alcohol, sex or gambling. My drug of choice was FOOD. I used food to self-medicate. If things went badly, I'd eat. If they went good, I'd eat. If I was depressed, I'd eat. My life revolved around food. I thought about food ALL the time.

The big breakthroughs for me came during group therapy. I had to confront some of the horrible things that happened to me as a child. The facilitator for our group would focus on one specific painful issue at a time. Then bring that issue it to a boiling point. I, as the client, would SCREAM what I was feeling at the top of my lungs. Lots of tears, swearing, and yelling at the person that hurt me. At other times they would have me BEAT a GIANT pillow with a bat, while yelling and crying. I would hit this pillow until I was totally exhausted and spent. Some of these sessions lasted 1–3 hours at a time. It was EXHAUSTING work! But each time I got GREAT relief and forgiveness.

I confronted one issue with lots of journaling. My mother was an alcoholic. She used to beat the crap out of me till I was black and blue for no reason other than I was walking too loud when she was trying to rest. I learned early on as a child to eat my way through uncomfortable situations and abuse.

At Shades of Hope, we went through a series of EXREMELY PAINFUL forgiveness exercises. Although my mother is no longer alive, I learned to forgive her and myself.

> *I am no longer a victim. With the help of my family, significant others, support group and great friends, I meet my challenges head on. Are my eating and food choices perfect? No, but I'm moving forward!*
>
> *To date I've lost 80 pounds. Completed 2 half Marathons. Climbed The Stratosphere Hotel Casino in Las Vegas. In June of 2012, I met a TEAM in Africa to climb Mount Kilimanjaro.*
>
> Robby LeBlanc,
> Author, Speaker, and Recording Artist
> www.RobbyLeBlanc.com

Mary's story, Robby's story, and June's story are those that we can all relate to in some way. If you have not experienced those issues yourself, you probably know someone close to you that has. No matter what the issues are, the commonality in all these stories, and in YOUR story, is that the thoughts you have about yourself can be very abusive and disempowering and have a great effect on your very happiness and self-esteem.

In this next story, this particular journey to self-forgiveness is a little harder to relate to. It will pull at your heartstrings and could easily fit into the chapter on forgiving the unforgivable or in the chapter on forgiving God. Yet, the path back to our true self is often the most treacherous one. Charlene's story teaches us that it is so easy to lose the preciousness of your loved ones. That a simple choice, one we make every day, can change our world forever. We all make mistakes. We have to learn to forgive ourselves for those mistakes. Yet, in this particular circumstance, there was no mistake made, no choice made that was any different than the choices made every single day. And often when there is no one to blame, the person is left to blame him/herself.

Charlene's Path to Self-Forgiveness

I am living testament to the lessons of self-forgiveness. I used to think that self-forgiveness was a destination on the road map to spirituality. Over the years, I have come to realize that for me, it is a continual state of being. Being in forgiveness . . . is a place of balance within me that brings every other aspect of my being into balance and alignment. I must practice self-forgiveness daily, similar to a person going through AA. This journey is about GA. Guilt Anonymous! There are still times when I must choose daily to forgive myself and move forward.

Forgiving others is far easier than forgiving yourself. I am my own worst critic. My story begins many years ago . . . with my birth. It may seem funny to go back that far, but I was put up for adoption when I was born. Even though I felt wanted by my "new" parents, I lacked true attachment as an infant and somewhere in the back of my psyche; I always wondered why I wasn't good enough for my bio-family. Especially since I was the only child, out of ten, placed for adoption. This burden always remained as a personal filter through which I poured all of the events of my personal life. It played havoc with my self esteem.

When I was in my mid 30's, my two youngest children and I were in a chemical spill on the way home from my work one day, and about 18 months later they developed acute forms of cancer. They passed over 13 months apart, at ages 3 and 5.

During the three years that my children were sick, and every year that has followed, I have found myself in rapid spiritual growth and wrestling with guilt, much like a juggling contest. Over the years, my wrestling matches with guilt have become less frequent. I find that I have grown spiritually and often can recognize the newest disguise that guilt clothes itself in, thus being able to rid myself of its harmfulness sooner. With every changing season, the focus of my growth has changed – the three biggest challenges were also my two biggest milestones: 1) making my peace with God, the creator; 2) forgiving myself for the events that led up to my daughter's and son's deaths; and 3) making peace with the fact that my other children suffered from my absence while I cared for their dying siblings.

As a professional working with families, I could reason that deaths of my children were not a direct result of something I had done. But as a mother, laying in the darkness of the night, I found myself bargaining countless times that "if I had just taken a different route home that day, we would have never been exposed to the chemical spill." Others have said to me "how could you have known there would be a spill on that road?" or "another route home would have taken you miles out of your way." All true, but nevertheless, as a mother you want to protect your children no matter what the cost.

Spending two weeks of each month in the hospital left my older children to adapt to being with other caretakers, or many times, my oldest daughter had to help with their care. This was agonizing for me. I was often faced with making decisions or choices utilizing less than desirable options. It felt to me as if I had to choose from 'the lessor of two evils' at times and that the older children lost something in each of the options.

Over the years I had come to the realization that I did the best I could with the options I had available to me, given the circumstances. But I'm here to tell you I have had to accept that as my position. Guilt can be very sophisticated and often lies dormant only to appear articulately and divisively when you least expect it. Much to my surprise, even though I am a trained professional, and had dealt extensively with the normal triggers in psychotherapy, I found myself dancing yet again, and again, with guilt – each time in a more highly transformed version.

I have also come to see that there are many opportunities for continued growth by facing my fears head on. It's only by the illumination, through being very honest with myself, in this personal quest for truth that I can measure my success or recognize an opportunity for trusting my heart and stepping forward through my fear, to cast light on my own "personal demons." I now look to past experience for strength or enlightenment, rather than suffering in silence.

I learned that you do not have to be "happy or glad" about something that happened in order to personally grow from it. In fact, big growth steps seldom come from easy or fun events in our personal lives. Once we take that first step, the second one will be a bit easier. I learned that if I keep going, over time we will be wiser and stronger!

Here is a poem I wrote many years ago. Perhaps it will comfort someone who is searching.

"In the safety and silence of this place I can sometimes hear the voice of my soul . . . telling me to trust the light in my heart.

True healing comes from within centering myself– so that the light within me continues to grow stronger and illuminates my path.

When I allow myself to be guided by spirit and . . . when I am able to listen, the gentle spirit voice speaks to me – of my own great strength reassuring me that if I can but let go . . .

It will lead me homeward to a place of healing."

Charlene Stutes
Family Advocacy Consultant
charlenestutes@yahoo.com

Charlene has experienced it all. Feeling guilt over what happened, she blamed herself, asking, "what if . . ." and ruminating, "if only . . . ." Her story is here because you as the reader can clearly and intelligently surmise, she did nothing wrong. Yet, I know your heart goes out to her as you too might have felt the same way. It is so important to step outside of yourself, become the objective observer of your life, and remove the guilt and shame that paralyzes you. Make the choice, right now, to release the guilt and shame and to allow the beauty of who you truly are to come through. In this way, you can be the gift to the world you were meant to be.

Shame and guilt do not change the situation, and certainly do not fix it. A spiritual awakening, in which you learn to let go of shame and guilt, and choose to replace them with self-love and forgiveness, can move mountains!

Adultery and Self-Forgiveness

Another area that is hard for self forgiveness is when a family is broken up as a result of adultery. The only way to "get over" adultery or another kind of hurt is to forgive and be forgiven. What gets in the way of this is often the ego. The ego can tell you many confusing things, such as you do not deserve to be forgiven, that you need to be punished, or that you really did nothing wrong. The EGO (Edging God Out) keeps us from facing the reality of the situation, taking personal responsibility, and learning the lessons we need to learn. The ego keeps us from loving ourselves enough to remember that we are human and we make mistakes from time to time. What we want most is to love and be loved. Yet, when the ego is in control, it keeps us from forgiving and being forgiven.

Unfortunately, self deception is often what gets in the way of a couple reconciling. Having the integrity to admit what happened and to take personal responsibility for what happened goes a long way in relationships. Rebuilding trust takes a lot of hard work. It takes a willingness to live your life as an open book. This can be used as a beautiful self-growth tool and a way to make a relationship even stronger. Unfortunately, that path is rarely taken. The truth is that it is easier to "stuff the pain" than to face it.

Of course, if you are the one who hurt someone else, you want to be forgiven. It eases your own guilt and pain when someone says, "I forgive you!" Receiving the forgiveness of someone else is like being given a second chance – a chance to prove your "goodness" and your "wholeness." Yet, the truth is, you are already whole! There are a million reasons for families to break up, and we rarely see the entire gift in any given situation until years later. If you are blamed for a marriage breaking up, you need to take personal responsibility for your part in the break up, and then you need to forgive yourself.

Our mistakes are just reminders that we have veered off course a bit.

We can always recalibrate and reset our course!

I have a friend who cheated on her spouse and asked him repeatedly for forgiveness. It's been years and he is still punishing her by withholding forgiveness. When she says it's time we move on, he accuses her of taking no responsibility for his hurt. She must move on and must not be defined by this one action, this one 'mistake'. I think it is a shame that he is letting his life be defined by this action on her part. She would love his forgiveness but has stopped asking for it. She has learned that she must forgive herself.

"Without being forgiven, released from the consequences of what we have done, our capacity to act would, as it were, be confined to a single deed from which we could never recover; we would remain the victims of its consequences forever, not unlike the sorcerer's apprentice, who lacked the magic formula to break the spell."

~ Hannah Arendt,
Jewish Philosopher, Author and Poet

I think if someone keeps blaming others for how hurt they feel, that they are ignoring their own piece of responsibility in the relationship. In my friend's case, her husband can continue to NOT deal with his own issues as long as he keeps blaming her for his hurts. Remaining a victim is never healthy. We are all responsible for our own feelings.

Learning to Heal the Heart Through Self-Forgiveness

If there is pain in your heart, you can build your walls to try to protect yourself from feeling the pain, or you can open your heart and know that you can heal your pain with self love and self forgiveness. Knowing that you can be hurt and can get over it is an extraordinary human gift that makes you stronger, builds your forgiveness muscle, and keeps you feeling grounded and protected. Spending a lifetime avoiding hurt keeps you from feeling passion, love, or joy. The heart has amazing qualities of healing, while living from the head/ego keeps you controlled and restricted. We want to be brave and courageous and allow our hearts to open and expand. To inspire you further, please get into a comfortable position and open your heart to Aazura's channeling of the

Divine Union of Magdalene and Jeshua:

And so we welcome all those that are available to listen to this message. We are excited for the openness of so many people in the world right now to the idea of forgiveness from a much different perspective. It isn't just about saying, it's okay, but it's about completely realigning the heart. It's about completely realigning the mind. For in the reality right now that is being created in this word, the mind is being shattered, the heart is being healed. It used to be the other way around. And so when people speak about forgiveness, they're beginning to really understand the depths of the meaning of this word – it is forgiving. It is "for giving" to oneself and to others the love that is necessary for the expansion of life, for the renewal of this world. Outside of forgiving there is contraction, let's say, and there is a holding back. There is a resistance, and the only real pathway to unconditional love is allowing.

Now, this does not mean that all actions occur in one's life are acceptable in a way that they can continue to harm one or another. For you always have the power of discernment of knowing what is right for you and what does not accompany you on your path and the direction you'd like to go. But you always have the choice to release the struggle, release the pain around any situation, but we would like to start with you forgiving yourself. Letting go of all ideas of what others have done, or not done. It is really about self-love – because you can honestly look at yourself and understand that all experiences are simply that. Somewhere within your own soul, it was conditioned to happen the way it did – based on your own perceptions, your own experiences, so that you might see something that may reflect to you love's opposite. It could be disappointment, it could be making a decision that you now judge wrong about yourself. There is no judgment in the mind of God. That is a personal experience through the experience of the world of duality. There is either acceptance and allowing, or judgments and resistance.

And so when one is forgiving to ones self, one is giving love to one's self, and you are all divine children of God. And this life's journey is all about experiences, and learning, and growing, and expanding. The act of forgiveness is the greatest opportunity for expansion and to a grander awareness and to a grander experience of life and to a deepening understanding of love and compassion. And when one lets go of the ideas of how one should be, freedom resides.

The "shoulds" are let go of when forgiveness has been allowed. So in the act of forgiveness when you are forgiving yourself, when you are coming back to loving yourself for all the struggle, all the pain, all the disappointments, all the abandonment, the lies, the mistrust, all the things that create ideas that one should be in resistance to something, someone, some experience, or one's self, the entire line all the way back to the beginning of that experience and into the future has been resolved and cleared. It is not just about that one situation. Humanity is beginning to understand the power of their own mind, the power of love in a new way. You are co-creators. And when you come back to forgiving one self, it has an exponential effect of all life around you that is honoring your God-self. And so when you do this for yourself, you impact all those around you. You impact the past, the present, changing the future.

So we encourage you to begin with the forgiveness at home, within your own heart. Love yourself enough to give yourself permission to feel that which is uncomfortable. Including the experiences, the pain, the struggles that one has some difficulty in letting go of. And as you begin to give yourself permission to feel into these expressions of energy and emotions, you change the course of history and the future. That is how powerful you are. So we invite you to come back home; to give to yourself the love that is always given to you, whether you can see it or not. You are enveloped always in grace, in love. Take this piece with you: all judgment is held within the mind of humanity, not the creator and because of that, you have the power and the freedom to change everything, just by forgiving yourself. That is what we've been waiting to say. You are loved deeply.

The Divine Union of Jeshua and Magdalene
Channeled through Aazura
www.NewHumanProject.com

In our society, we have allowed religious and other leaders to take the lead of whether to punish or absolve our guilt. The priest at confession gives absolution. The parole board decides whether you paid your debt to society. Our parents decide if our apology was good enough. The truth is YOU do not need to be absolved of your guilt by anyone else. Since God does not judge us and loves us unconditionally, please know that you already ARE absolved of all guilt. Of course, there is nothing wrong with feeling peace from these practices, and if you do, continue them. I understand that sometimes it is nice to know that someone else sees you as whole, not flawed, and forgivable. I am here to gently remind you to remember and to accept that God is inside of you, that being hurt and hurting others are human traits, and that we all share in the flow of feeling hurt, hurting others and finding forgiveness. It is basically all about letting go of self-judgment.

~~~***~~~
~~~

Living with Forgiveness Process

Step 1. Acknowledgment and Acceptance: Living forgiveness means letting yourself off the hook and stopping the repeated and incessant self-abuse. It means somehow doing what Mary, June, Robby and Char did here by accepting where they were and then making the decision, "I don't like where I am, so I am going to do something to change!" Change starts from the place of knowing where we are when we begin, and then having a vision of where we want to be. There is a certain reality each person had to face, and it takes an act of courage to deal with it head on.

Step 2. Personal Responsibility: Anybody who has been in a situation where they spent years beating themselves up knows that this does not create happiness. You might have heard others say, "You need to love yourself." OK, where do I start? What does that mean? How do I do it? Where is the roadmap?

Every journey starts with one step. It is necessary to take one step that is different from all the other steps you have taken thus far. Throughout this chapter, you have read many suggestions. Try one of these right now:

– Say the word "No" more often. Stop trying to please others.

– Give yourself the gift of "good enough" and stop searching for perfection. It is not there.

– When a negative, self-abusive thought comes in, notice it and change your focus. Don't spend time dwelling on it and trying to prove it correct.

– Play with boundaries, what feels comfortable, and what does not. Speak your truth out loud.

– If you want to make a life changing plan, hire a coach, go to a support group, or have a friend help you with an action plan. Take one step at a time and know it will take you approximately one month to create a new habit.

– If you are racked with guilt, I want you to be your own loving parent and write yourself a letter telling yourself how much you are loved and why you are so loved.

– Create a spiritual practice for yourself and connect with Spirit more often.

– Build your forgiveness muscle by forgiving yourself and others every single day for tiny things.

Step 3. Finding the Gift: For many people forgiving themselves and releasing guilt and shame, this is gift enough. Not living a self-abusive relationship with yourself feels like total freedom. For me, learning to love myself was the gift. Learning to stand up for myself and speak my own truth, without backing down, was a gift. After a while, I even learned how to do it with grace rather than as a bossy self-righteous person. It is hard to create boundaries when you don't know how and it takes practice. If you sound mean or bitchy, look at it as another gift to keep building your forgiveness muscle and forgive yourself. Let it go every day.

Step 4. Gratitude: I feel blessed that my life is within my spiritual control rather than my ego's control. It was my ego that wanted me to feel bad about my weight or what I looked like. It was my ego that said I was not good enough and not smart enough. Now I know I am good enough. I am a perfectly lovable child of God. God does not make mistakes. I am not a mistake. Here is what I learned: I do not need to be fixed. Can you learn that about yourself? You might want to make changes, but you are not broken. Feel the gratitude daily that you can have the life you want to have. That you have the power to change if you desire. What a blessing that is!

Letting go of guilt and shame is most likely the greatest thing anyone can do on the road to self-enlightenment. You might just want to re-read this chapter. You will also find some Forgiving Self Meditations on my website, as well as in chapter 10. Remember, self-forgiveness is a continual process, and it is one that gets easier as we build our forgiveness muscle.

Chapter 8

Forgiving God

"Somewhere along the road, I found out that God wasn't the one creating all the pain in my life. I realized that my soul had chosen the experiences of growing up in an alcoholic home, being an alcoholic, being an unwed mother and not raising my son, having health problems, struggling with low self-worth, being in and out of dysfunctional relationships, and being in a career that was not the norm. My soul wanted to gain wisdom from each experience. God never stepped in and stopped me from learning lessons, but God did step in (when I asked) and helped me get through each of them. When I really understood that it wasn't God creating the pain in my life, but instead those experiences were life lessons my soul chose, my prayers changed and my relationship with God continued to change and heal."

~ Echo L. Bodine,
Echoes of the Soul:
Moving Beyond the Light
by Echo L. Bodine and
Nick Bunick (New World Library 1999)

This just might be the most controversial chapter I will ever write. I mean, who am I to talk about God? What do I know about God? I guess to have any validity here, I need to tell you my views and if you don't agree, then maybe this chapter will not work for you, or maybe it will work even if we see things differently, I'll leave that up to you, my dear reader.

Here it is. God is love. God is both mother and father, neither male nor female. God is both a noun and a verb. God loves us unconditionally. We don't have to go through any intermediary to find or communicate with God, because God is inside all of us. God shows up in us as spirit.

Our human life is tough because we left the place where we know we are part of God and we miss God. We miss God a lot! We feel lost and at times, lonely and afraid. Not having that 100% connection for us humans is a tough path. I believe as children we remembered that we are spirit and eventually we forgot.

As small human children, our parents, the people who feed us and take care of us, become our Gods. Unfortunately, no one told them what they needed to do and their love often times did not feel unconditional or non-judgmental, like God's love would feel. Thus we felt the intensity of being separated from God and alone in the world.

The bottom line is we miss God. We are taught many things about how to get to God. We try to be good, and then God will love us (oops, that was our parent's rules). We go to church, mosque, or temple and try to connect through the leader who we are told is an emissary to God. We go through various rituals and ceremonies and we pray. We do as we are told by our religious leaders and parents, and often we still feel like something is missing.

Our relationship with God becomes an issue when something unexpected happens in our life, shaking our foundation to the core. Someone abandons or rejects us, someone dies unexpectedly, someone commits what we'd call a sin, or we do something that we would call a sin and feel shame or guilt over it. Our belief or disbelief in God comes to a head often when there is no one else to blame and we can not bear the pain. We feel left, forsaken, and abandoned by God. We blame God. And we hate it when someone says, "God does not give us more than we can handle!" The truth is, we've had enough and we do not want to keep 'handling' anything.

Our belief in God comes to a head when there is no one else left to blame.

Often, we try to bargain with God. I remember when my first husband was hit by a car just a few months after we were married. His lung was punctured and I had no idea what would happen. Intellectually, at that time, I said I didn't believe in God. I thought that God was just a crutch for needy people. Seriously, that is what I believed! Well, I became needy and instantly started bargaining. "Please God don't let him die. I promise I'll be good. I'll be a better wife. I'll work harder . . . ." I honestly don't even remember the bargains I made, but I know they went on for a long time over those first two days. I hedged my bets, just in case there was a God. I wanted my bases covered.

I have to admit, I feel rather embarrassed writing all of this, as now I am deeply spiritual, and I hope I do not treat God like a spiritual tool to wheel and deal with. If I do, however, I am sure He[26] will forgive me, unconditionally.

Loss and Suicide

Suicide and loss of a child are some of those times when we really get down on our hands and knees and rage at God. How could this happen to me! What did I do? We bargain, we beg, we wish and we pray for things to be different, for our pain to be taken away. In an earlier chapter, you were introduced to Christine whose four month old daughter passed away in day care. You know she must have had many discussions with God in the following days, months and years. Interestingly, she became closer to God, and more spiritual, than she was before the death.

My friend Shelly, lost a child to suicide. A double whammy. A good person, someone who LOVES being a mother and blamed herself, and God, for not being able to protect her precious son.

A regression session, years after his death, helped her to realize her son is on the other side, and is fine and he wants her to stop punishing herself.

Shelly's Story:

> *The morning of October 1, 2006 started out like any other Sunday. I had been trying to reach my son Casey down in Mesa and he hadn't returned my call, so I was a little annoyed, I knew he was working that day, so he would probably call me from there. Maybe something was wrong with his cell phone. I asked his brother to check on him the day*

before, he went to his apartment and there was no answer.

The day went on, I didn't hear from him. I tried his work number again but got his voice mail, he was probably busy.

Around 7:00 that night, with still no call, my husband convinced me to call the police to go and check up on him. I called his brother to tell him what I had done and he agreed to go over there too.

Soon after, the police called. This was the start of our nightmare, my precious, beloved son had taken his life.

The days following were filled with pain, numbness and questions. The following days brought revelations about Casey's life that we didn't know about. He was health conscious and intelligent, yet, he chose to try steroids. For his emotional troubles, he made another poor choice, alcohol and drugs to numb his pain.

Of course the first things a mother asks are "how could he do this to his family?" "Why couldn't he turn to us with his problems?" "What could possibly cause him to take such a permanent and terrible step?" "I'm his MOTHER, why didn't he come to me?"

I came to the conclusion that Casey did what he did in a terrible, split-second fit of rage.

There were signs in his bedroom that pointed to this. He didn't leave a note.

No matter what and no matter how many unknowns, we were left to deal with the aftermath. I have done a great deal of reading on the subject of being a parent of a child who dies by suicide and there is always a section or two about dealing with the anger and how to forgive your child. The strange thing is that, for me, those chapters didn't help. I never felt any anger towards Casey that required forgiveness. I only felt profound sadness, loss and despair.

As I thought about writing this, I realized that my anger, and therefore, the need for forgiveness was with ME. What kind of a mother was I that my child took this step? Why didn't he feel he could come to me? What a colossal failure I was in a role that I thought was the most important thing I could do with my life, being a mother!!! How could I ever face myself and the world?

The truth is, each time I have to tell someone the circumstances of Casey's death and even when I look in the mirror, I feel deep shame as a mother. I think others are judging me.

When my oldest son had his first child, I was afraid my heart was so dead I would not be able to love him as I should. Fortunately, I discovered, I can still love and my grandchildren are the lights of my life.

As I search my heart to write this, I realize I do not feel worthy of happiness or peace. If I knew whether Casey was at peace, maybe I could find it in myself. All of this has taken a toll on my marriage. I have only taken 4 days off work in the last two years, as I feel I don't deserve to be happy.

I realize I'm feeling the same guilt as maybe a serial killer might. I'm not a terrible or heinous person. I can give to others, just not myself. I know the clichés, "if you can't love yourself, you can't love anyone else or no one will be able to love you!" I know my husband and family deserve to have me as a happy person in their lives. How do I start?

I realize that the first step is to accept that I am not perfect and trying for perfection is ridiculous. I need to accept that of course I made mistakes as a parent, but NEVER on purpose. Maybe I could help others to learn from any mistakes I may have made and learn to not just survive, but to live again.

I believe that Casey would want me to try to find peace and forgive myself. I know this is a long and arduous path for me. But it has been five years, I need to try.

In order to try, I did a past life regression, which put me into a trance. I saw myself having a totally peaceful life, and understood the purpose of being shown that lifetime was to let me know I CAN live in peace, with the love of my family who is here on earth with me.

Because I was in a deep trance, I was able to clearly connect with Casey. He is not suffering at all. He was smiling and hugging me and told me it is OK! He told me it was beyond my control and that I am not responsible for everything that goes on! He said he had an illness and that he would not have listened to me anyway.

My sister who recently passed also came and said I do deserve happiness. It was always a contest between us to see who was the saddest. She said she wasted a lot of time being unhappy. I was told to say "no" to others, and start saying "yes" to myself. The bottom line is that I need to have a happy life and not be afraid of being happy.

Now that I know Casey is happy and safe, and doesn't blame me, I believe I can let go of the self-pity blame game. I am ready to take the reins of control back on my life. It was a great gift to know that he is ok. Now, I can breathe.

Shelly Collier
Cottonwood, Arizona

You can see that Shelly's story could be in almost any chapter here. But with these kinds of losses, it's easy to blame everyone and everything. We fortunately live in a time where we are waking up to realize that we are in charge of the happiness or sadness of our own lives. Hopefully, Shelly can take the advice of loved ones from the other side and let herself, and God, off the hook and start enjoying the good things her life still has to offer.

I am not going to talk about spiritual redemption here, or about God forgiving us, because there is no doubt in my mind that forgiveness is a human issue, and that God loves us unconditionally. That means NO CONDITIONS. (Remember Immaculée Ilibagiza's story in chapter 6, when she was stuck in the bathroom listening to a baby being murdered outside the window? God told her that the child, as well as the murderers, were all his children. That is the kind of non-judgment and acceptance I am talking about.) We are not even able to comprehend what that means, because the truth is that we all have conditions, expectations and judgments.

When do you get angry with God?

When do you get angry with God?

When do you get angry with God?

When your life does not go the way you want it to go. When you feel so much pain that there is no one left to blame. You already blamed everyone you could think of, including yourself, and still you feel no peace. You blame God when what happened seems so unfair, so unjust, so unthinkable, so unforgivable, so painful, so unbelievable, or so unspeakable that you just cannot bear the pain anymore.

I know it's sad. I know it doesn't really make sense. But it is true.

We don't want to admit doing this. It seems so messy. So unspiritual. We are supposed to love God. God is supposed to love us. Why would She hurt us in this way? We get angry with God because She does not do things the way we want them done.

Free Will

Oh, it's at this time we conveniently forget about free will! That's right. We live in a universe of free will, where God says I love you but you are in charge of your own life! God does not interfere in our lives, in our plans, or in our soul contracts.

Our soul contracts? What are those?

As a soul regression therapist, I have come to learn that we all have a plan before we come to this earth school. Yes, it is true that we are all connected by the life-force of God and Oneness. Yet we are also individual souls with a plan to progress through various stages, to evolve, and to become self-actualized.[27] When planning on coming into human form, we decide what we want to accomplish and what lesson(s) our soul would like to learn. Sometimes it takes one lifetime, sometimes many, to learn particular lessons. We get to choose our parents, siblings, lovers, spouses and children. We get to choose our body, our sex, our cultural background, our medical conditions, our looks, our class level, what country and continent we are born on, etc. We have plans and back-up plans. We have fork-in-the-road plans. If I turn left this will happen. If I turn right that will happen. We have contingencies if we get off track. And ultimately, we have free will to not follow any plan at all and ignore it all.

Concurring with this view, in the book, *Your Soul's Plan: Discovering the Real Meaning of the Life You Planned Before You Were Born* (2009) by Robert Schwartz, clients in regression talk about the soul's plans: "From the viewpoint of the soul, no event or course of action is "bad." All is simply experience, and every experience teaches and offers seeds of growth." "Not learning a lesson is not failure," declared Doris's soul. "Think of it more as choosing to learn it on a different path. Anything can be judged, and anything can be seen from a non-judgmental and compassionate level."

We could choose to come to earth to help a soul friend/mate of ours learn their lesson. We could come here for a short period of time, or a longer period of time. The book *Spiritual Psychology: The Twelve Primary Life Lessons* (2004) by Steve Rother describes 12 common lessons that people come here to learn. My intuition tells me there are many more lessons, but if you can not arrange to have your own soul regression,[28] then this is a good place to start to learn more about your particular life lesson.

A question often asked is "why would I choose such a difficult life?" Actually, it sounds more like this: "there is no f-ing way I would have chosen this!" People often wonder if they are being punished by God to have the life they have chosen – it must be karmic payback[29] for being really awful in a past life. I believe it's less random than that, that we do have quite a bit of input into our life choices.

Someone might ask, if I was born blind, is that karma? My gut tells me it is more likely YOU chose not to see for other reasons, like developing your inner spiritual life, to be more focused on self, or to learn to be less attached to how things look to other people, etc. There could be 100 other reasons to choose blindness.

There are so many beautiful lessons we learn. I have two friends who gave birth to Down-syndrome children when they were both very young women. Both were shocked, scared, filled with fear at the time. Both would tell you today that these children were truly a gift from God, angels who bring love and light daily to their families and their community. At the time something unexpected or unplanned happens, it's easy to blame God. That is OK, God can handle it. Then, we can remember that there is a reason for everything, even if we can't see it at the time. We can remember the "why" will be revealed later.

What about being abused as a child? Could this be karma? Yes. Could there be 100 other reasons? Yes. Perhaps you wanted to learn how to stick up for yourself or how to develop boundaries at a young age. Maybe you wanted to learn to love yourself and created the opposite by being raised to feel unlovable so you could overcome it and learn the lessons of self-love. Remember, we are on a planet of duality. So, often we learn our lessons through paradoxes – through experiencing the opposite of what we want. We humans actually love the overcoming of things. It's the ultimate hero's journey. You are reading this book so I know you also long to forgive, to overcome your past experiences, and find peace in your future. Am I correct? We are so blessed in this day and age to have the awareness, the mindfulness to be able to observe our own life and choose to fix or change the things we are not happy with.

Earth is a fantastic school. *A Course in Miracles* teaches us that Earth is an agreed upon hallucination. We are all part of the illusion. Only our lives as spiritual beings is real. This is a lot to get our minds around, but let's just play with this for a minute. Whether this is a hallucination or not, it is something we chose to have as an experience, so why not make the best of it? Why not step into it completely and fully and learn every single nugget we can from the experience we chose in this lifetime? If we do not learn this lesson, we will come back to relearn it in the future. DANG! I don't want to come back and play the same game again, do you? I am choosing to really step up and learn it all right now and be done with these life lessons. How about you?

Learning to forgive God comes into play, I believe, when we have really tough experiences to overcome. As I said earlier, dealing with a suicide, or loss of a loved one, are definitely some of those situations where we start asking, "Why God, why?" The next story, from my friend Becca, illustrates how you can move from such despair and such pain to find peace through forgiveness.

Healing from Suicide, Learning to Forgive EVERYONE

Knowing the difficulties of approaching forgiveness takes on an additional challenge when that person has transitioned from this world. It takes on a greater complexity when the forgiveness surrounds the person for taking their own life.

It was January 28, 1999, when I came home to find my husband hanging from the basement rafters by his favorite neck tie. After calling 911, getting him down, and doing CPR to find that the EMS techs immediately declared him dead, I was left traumatized.

I went into a world of chain smoking and numbness that lasted for over 3 months. I worked to breathe. I ate and drank only because I knew that it would only get worse, whatever "it" was. I even thought that maybe this world was too difficult, too mean and too bad and that maybe my husband had it right . . . to end my life would be to end the pain of this world and his death.

With family, friends and great medical intervention, I eventually began to thaw from the numbness. With the thaw came the next levels of emotions which eventually lead to feelings of betrayal, of abandonment and of pain. It also led to the dichotomy of loving him while hating what he did to me and himself, not to mention the feelings of anger and hatred toward God.

As I look back now, I realize that one of the first steps to forgiveness is to realize that forgiveness does not include forgetting. There would never be the bliss of amnesia around this trauma. The events of that fateful day would forever be etched in my memory bank. What I didn't realize then, was that how I remember those events had a lot to do with the forgiveness work I had yet to do.

I remember the exact moment of turnaround. I was driving to work as I broke into tears saying "I want to live" The next part was to not just exist, but truly to live a purposeful happy life again. This meant forgiveness . . . forgiveness of my husband's actions; forgiveness of myself for not being there to save him; forgiveness for not wanting to interact with him the morning of that fateful day; forgiveness to myself for falling in love with and marrying an alcoholic; forgiveness in being a great co-dependent; and eventually, forgiveness of God.

How do you forgive when you never have forgiven anything of this magnitude? You get the help, advice and support in any way possible. I worked with my medical doctor, my counselors, and my psychiatrist. I got support from my family, friends, and co-workers. I fed my soul at the local Unity church. Eventually I started reading self-help books, listened to self-help audios and went to self-help seminars. Each opened my mind, and eventually my heart, to do the work ahead of me. No matter how much you read, listen to or attend, you eventually have to do your own work to heal.

To list everything I did, would take a book. Each tool I learned and used eventually became part of my integrative clinic and is part of the work I now do to help others heal traumas. The first thing that is core to forgiving is to talk as if you have what you want. I wanted to heal and be happy again. I can't even tell you how hard that was at first. How do you say the words knowing in your heart that it is not what you are feeling? Eventually, you believe what you say as you manifest your forgiveness and your happiness. Through journaling, seminars, counseling, prayer, and deep introspection, I not only forgave my husband, I forgave myself and I forgave God.

For me, it wasn't about holding on to the pain of the past or the need for paybacks or revenge. With my husband's death, there was no revenge or getting back. There was only the choice of living in the pain of the past or doing anything possible to heal the wound and finding happiness in my new life ahead of me.

I can't tell you the process was easy. I would never want anyone to go through what I did. I can tell you that it was worth it in that it has made me grow beyond my imagination. I have grown personally, professionally and spiritually. I have tools in my personal tool belt that have come in handy for other traumas since then, especially when I got sick and I almost died 4 times.

I forgave so well, that after I moved from Michigan to Arizona following my passion in healing work, I created an award winning integrative clinic, I lived a very happy life out of the shadow of my husband's suicide. Almost five years after my husband died, during a meditation group I was leading, he came to me. After the meditation, as we shared, there were 12 of the 13 people who were visited by a deceased loved one during the meditation. As we all are synchronistic, there was healing that occurred for each of us. As my husband stood in front of me, he said that he was all healed now. He then opened a door and it revealed a classroom with people sitting at desks working on papers. As I looked in, my husband told me that he now helps heal the people on the other side like him that have taken their own lives. In my heart, I felt the wholeness around his life and his suicide.

By forgiving, I ultimately healed from the suicide of my husband and I believe it lead to the healing of my husband on the other side. I also found that by letting go of the weight of the trauma and pain through forgiveness, I actually opened myself up to creating a happy life, living an adventure and following my passion.

If we really come into this world to learn lessons, I believe that we agree to the lesson but do not know the way we are going to learn the lesson. I believe that my husband and I were destined to come together and to marry. He came into my life so that I could learn to heal and to demonstrate through my own life, that through forgiveness, everyone can find a life beyond any trauma. For that I am very grateful.

I now work in many ways to teach others how to heal through the worst traumas in their lives to find the happiness they deserve.

Becca Tokarczyk, PT, M.Ed., IHT-MP
Beyond Grief, LLC
www.LifeBeyondSuicide.com

I realize that Becca's process might not be your process. I often tell clients that they must be very advanced to choose such tough, intense lessons. Advanced souls, when creating their contracts, believe they can handle anything and they know that nothing is impossible. They are fully aware of all the ramifications and possibilities and have faith that they will come out the other side.

You

You are not
Just a body
With a Soul
Inside.
You are a Soul
Gift-wrapped
With a body.[30]

So, we are sad and miserable and we don't know what to do. We get mad at God for not protecting us from this hurt. We deserve better don't we? Weren't we good enough? Bad things are not supposed to happen to good people right? Wrong. If we chose our lessons, then these things were supposed to happen and if they were supposed to happen, then they must be happening either for our benefit, our soul friend's benefit, or the benefit of our community.

Here are some questions to ponder as we process our anger or disappointment in God. What if God is actually respecting our plan and knows what is in the whole contract? What if He is honoring our soul's wishes? What if God just stays out of the way of our earthly decisions and leaves it up to us? Wow, that's a scary thought! What if we are in fact in charge of the outcome of the Earth! Do you think God creates wars? Do you think God takes sides? Do you think God loves one group of people more than any other group? Is there a particular group you think God hates?[31]

What do we do with this and what does it have to do with forgiveness?

Doesn't it make sense that if we are all spirit pieces of God, then God certainly must care about the pieces of Herself? Think of God as your higher spiritual command center and ask what God would do, or ask for God's guidance. This does not mean you will be treated like a spoiled child or brat and will get everything you want! Don't think you can fool God by using prayer as a bargaining chip. It does not work that way. Think of it more like you are igniting your God-spark inside of you. Do not judge your relationship with God on whether you get everything you ask for. All we can really ask for is our ultimate gift from God – the spiritual growth of our soul. A good prayer to use is: Dear God, please allow me to wake up and understand why this is happening to me, or accept that it is ok for me not to know at this point in my life. Help me handle this situation with grace and compassion, especially for myself. Help me to breathe when I want to give up. Help me take my anger and frustration and fear and turn it into love and acceptance. Please show me the next step. Thank you. And so it is, Amen, Amen, Amen.

If you are angry at God because you didn't get your way or because something was not fair, then stomp your feet, yell, scream, and get it out of your system and get on with your life. If you can possibly remind yourself that you were a willing participant in this life plan, then maybe it will help you take personal responsibility for your part in this creation.

You love God and you want God to be on your side and to help you through hard times. I understand that. But know that you also have guides and angels who have come to be with you throughout your earth journey. They are there for you. They help you when you request help. Think of them as God's helpers on earth. Better yet, think of them as your helpers on earth. Your contract includes these spiritual helpers whom you love and trust.[32] When you pray to God, they are also included in your prayers and they hear you and do their best to help you. Please be warned though, they are not here to interfere in your life but only when you ask for help, so ask for help. Their job is to help you. Please keep them employed.

Living with Forgiveness Process

Step 1. Acknowledgment and Acceptance: Living forgiveness means stepping into the truth of what we created, and at the same time realizing the paradox of it not being reality at all. Imagine asking God to get you the job you want and then it turns out you hate the job. Do you blame God? What about when you do not get the job, do you blame God even though you don't know that six months later something better is going to come along?

We need to acknowledge what we are upset about. Feel the feelings, because they are real. Just do not get stuck there! Do not allow the emotions to run you for any real length of time. In fact, you can even set a deadline. "I will feel sorry for myself and blame everyone, even God, for the next 24 hours!" And then move on.

Accept that you have no idea what God's plans are, or what your soul contract and plans are. Accept that you are only exposed to a small piece of the entire "story" and that God and your guides and angels are watching out for you. If you don't think they are, just give them a reminder. They won't mind. In fact, most of our guides and angels feel like they are in the unemployment lines. They are bored and they want something to do.

Becca could never have known that she and her husband had an agreement to help others deal with suicide on both sides of the veil, and that they needed to experience it before they could be good teachers.

Step 2. Personal Responsibility: How do you take responsibility when there is a seemingly untimely death or a disabling physical or mental disease? You can ask for guidance to seek the truth. Freedom comes with both accepting personal responsibility as well as the truth. Accepting personal responsibility in this case means personal responsibility for how you are RESPONDING to the situation, not that you caused it.

I just want to give you a little example from my own personal life so you know what I am talking about. My dog, Schuyler died at age 6. I blamed my ex-husband who took the dog, his wife, and yep, God. Schuyler was my champion. He got me through my divorce and watched over my children. I gave him to my ex because I knew he'd be happier where we used to live, up on a mountain where he could roam the hillside freely. He was suddenly sick and died within 48 hours of being taken to the vet.

My old story: He died of a broken heart because he was made to sleep outside instead of inside with the family, while the new wife's animals slept indoors.

My new truth: His time was simply up. He did what he came to earth to do, to love me and my children through a tough divorce. The day I found out about my ex's affair, I was crying and contemplating killing myself. Schuyler snuggled up with me on the floor and didn't leave my side. Every night for over a year, he would check on each of the children after they went to bed, put his nose right up to their little faces and then come and sleep in my room. He was the man of the house and served a great purpose in our lives. I believe he is an angel watching out for the kids to this day.

Step 3. Finding the Gift: Continuing with the example above, the gift was for me to accept that it was no one's fault. It was just time. The gift is in Schuyler's life and the memories we all had. For me, I was able to be very loving and less selfish by getting an opportunity to say to my ex-husband that he could have the dog a couple years after the divorce. It was a gift for me to be selfless and put Schuyler's desires ahead of my own. He was miserable in the small yard I had for him at my new house, and the ability to run the mountain was a blessing for him. I know that.

Can you see how I was able to take what could be a tragedy and turn it into a gift? You can do this too.

In the case of suicides and loss of loved ones, find the lessons as the gifts. What joy did they bring to your life? Can you now really cherish other loved ones in your life? How do you live your life differently as a result of unexpectedly losing a loved one? Use these questions for other times you blame God, like an accident causing a traumatic disfigurement or disability, or the loss of someone's mental/brain function. Whenever you start blaming God, ask how you have grown as a result of this situation.

Step 4. Gratitude: I feel blessed to have had the love of a dog like Schuyler. I had always been afraid of large dogs, but Schuyler was the most loving beautiful German Shepherd you could ask for. I can so clearly see him taking care of all of us and that kind of unconditional love is probably as close to the love of God as you get here on earth! Schuyler's job was complete and I am grateful he was in my life.

When we remember, as Tony Robbins says, that "Life happens not to me, but for me," we can't forget that we know how to turn hardship into blessings.

A Short Visualization

> Take a deep breath please, right now, and remember a time when something happened to you. Something so big that you blamed God! You were so angry at God and the world! Remember that time. It might have been the loss of a loved one. You might have been permanently disfigured, raped, abused, abandoned, or used. Whatever it was, remember it now and feel those feelings of loss, despair, desperation, anger, fear, or

devastation. Take another deep breath and now acknowledge and accept what happened.

Ask God what happened. Ask God what happened that you did not know about at the time. Hear and know the answer. What is the truth? Take it in, breath it into you. Feel the truth. If you need to, take responsibility. What was your piece in this story? Now, take another deep breath and know what the gift is/was. There is always a gift. Don't stop until you find it. If you cannot find it on your own, ask God or your guides and wait for an answer. After you know the gift, feel gratitude for the gift. Really take it in. It's ok to cry. Place your hands on your heart, feel the gift, feel gratitude, and feel "Thank you!" This is gratitude. This is what Forgiveness feels like. This is Living Forgiveness.

Chapter 9

When Forgiveness Isn't Enough

Creating Boundaries with the Habitual Offender

> "I've never met anyone with a perfect upbringing. It seems to me that life on planet Earth just doesn't work that way. The basic challenges of getting our needs met and managing boundaries are inherent in growing up human."
>
> ~ David Simon

Forgiving the past is so important.

However, what do you do when it's the present that needs to be forgiven? What do you do when someone, especially a family member, keeps re-offending? Have you ever been in a position where you wanted peace and you wanted to forgive a repeat offender, but you just could not do it? This is such an important area to address, because people feel guilty when they are unable to forgive.

As a life coach, the two main questions my clients ask regarding forgiving the repeat offender are, "What about the concept of *for better or worse*?" and, when it comes to their parents, "How can I possibly cut off my parents? They are my parents!" "But they are my children!" And then there are all the people who say "love has no boundaries and should have no boundaries."

Honestly, these are really tough questions. We are supposed to honor our parents, stay with our spouses, and advocate forever for our children. Tough love, co-dependency, and Al-Anon groups have sprung up all over in the last 30 years. Yet, it pains us to make these decisions. You might remember me speaking about my mother in Chapter 4, and how she was diagnosed with Cushing's Syndrome. I was just about ready to make the big decision to cut her out of my life. After years and years of emotionally draining me, I was ready to give up. Every conversation with her was emotionally taxing on me. It was like a Pavlov conditioning experiment: the phone would ring, it would be my mother and within one minute I was in the kitchen eating!

The day after the operation she was a totally different person. Her self-centeredness and obsessive behavior disappeared instantly. I can now talk to her on the phone without eating or pulling my hair out. I am able to forgive her because I recognize the behavior that really affected me was in the past. Although she still frustrates me, her behavior does not suck me dry. How do I handle boundaries? I give myself permission not to answer the phone every time she calls, I limit my calls to once a week, and I get off the phone quickly if I feel tension.

Most of us have some parent issues, for sure. You might recall that I also spoke earlier about my dad. As I went through the years with him, I held on to a lot of hurt and finally, I learned that blaming him for my hurts only hurt me. It kept me a victim. Yet, the one thing I had to face, and this was hard for me, was that even though I was able to forgive, I couldn't totally trust him. I call this the "YOU DO NOT HAVE TO BE NAÏVE" forgiveness myth. (See Chapter 2) My relationship with him is that we speak about once a month and I see him once a year. These boundaries work for me.

The universe is just so right on when there are issues left over that need to be healed. You will love this – right in the middle of writing this chapter of the book, I went and visited my family. During the visit, I was talking about this book and how I had forgiven him. His response was to simply rewrite our history at the dinner table and tell me he had always been there for me. I just sucked it up and didn't say anything except, "I know, Dad." He is getting old and I have no idea how long he is going to be around. I do not want to argue with him. The truth is, he was never there for me during any difficult times. My BODY remembered the FEELINGS/EMOTIONS of trying to please him and forgo my own needs. I learned that not saying anything was not in fact grace, but a denial of my truth. This is not about blaming him; it's about selling myself short, again. The back is all about integrity, and my words and beliefs were NOT in alignment. Can you see that? The old injury was triggered and it was my wake up call to heal another layer.

A few days later, I was down for the count, out on my back. The chiropractor I saw told me this was an "emotional" issue, with physical ramifications of course. Now, you might remember that my back issues began when I was with my father 25 years ago. I understood that by denying my feelings I once again allowed him to violate my boundaries by not standing up for myself! Just like I did 25 years ago. Do you see how complicated and deep all of this is? This is why we get triggered over and over again, to give us opportunities to heal the past and truly forgive. So, another layer of the onion for me! I did my EFT with the help of my chiropractor, and the living with forgiveness process. I took personal responsibility for my part in my story, found the gift and am grateful that YOU get to learn from this experience!

I'd like you to try to put your words/beliefs and actions together to re-align your situation. Go back to that incident and have it go in a way that does honor you. See the scene and hear the language being spoken back and forth and feel that new feeling in your body. If you need help, ask your angels and guides to help you with this process.

If we do not hear the calling of our soul to do something empowering, then our bodies may get involved. They "speak" to us through aches and pains, injuries and sometimes illnesses. What my body was saying was "slow down, and before you can move forward, do work on the issues with your father." A local Sedona healer helped me by reminding me to FEEL my FEELINGS (do you remember me suggesting this earlier in the book?) and then to rewrite the story. So for me, I am auditory (as opposed to visual or kinesthetic) and I rewrote the earlier hurts. I could hear my dad telling me "that's alright, you don't have to go on that ride, I didn't mean to push you sweetheart. What would you like to do?" And then I saw him put his arms around my shoulders and walk away from space mountain. Just imagining this happening helps me to breath. I went through about 3 other incidents with him that just really hurt me to my core and rewrote them too. The next day, I have to tell you, I felt about 80% better.

I have a client who also has a dad who is a repeat offender. He lies about things all the time. She can't trust what he says. He loves her, but he is not honest. And there were many times when that interfered in her marriage. She has forgiven him, but she can't really 'trust' him.

I have a client whose mother is a repeat offender. She is constantly putting her down. Her religious roots tell her she must honor her mother. Yet, they get into a screaming match every time they are together. She feels that her mother not only does not love her, but really doesn't even like her. Yet, she is somehow obligated to her and must be the good, obedient daughter. She is considering setting boundaries with her mother.

What about the woman whose husband is abusing her? A Christian take on this might be to "turn the other cheek" and to forgive and forget and ask God to make you a better wife. I say NO. If the cycle of abuse is being **repeated** in a marriage, a parent-child relationship, an employee-employer relationship, etc., this is not the time to turn the other cheek. If forgiveness is NOT stopping the abuse, then ask for the strength to get out safely and leave the relationship.

What about verbal abuse? What should you do when someone is just making your life miserable? Again, ask for and expect the miracle. The request is for the abusive behavior to end or for the strength to leave.

What about addiction issues? People struggle with this all the time. How do you rectify "for better or worse" when there is an addiction issue that is destroying your entire life or the lives of your children? Sometimes following societal or religious dictates actually destroy the very fabric of personal self-esteem. We might choose to do what is considered the "right thing" rather than making the difficult, painful and unpopular decision of setting boundaries and self-protection.

I am an advocate of creating your own future. Forgiveness is an important step in creating a healthy future, yet physical and emotional safety comes first. We will talk more about abuse in a few pages, but for now, remember that boundaries are needed, and then forgiveness can come.

Physical and Emotional Safety First.
Create and Set Boundaries.
Then you can Forgive.

Putting up and fortifying walls and not trusting others are absolutely NOT what I am advocating. What I am advocating is something called

Boundaries!

I think it is important to have a little boundary primer before we talk about creating boundaries and its relationship to forgiveness. The first step is to examine the concept of knowing your own boundaries and creating boundaries FOR YOURSELF. I discovered that if we start 'practicing' having clear boundaries in our daily lives, then creating the tough boundaries with those whom we love will be easier.

Self-care

To create a boundary, you need to first know what it is you need. Please go through this process with me and let's see if we can find the clarity together.

First, we start with the basics, your foundational needs. What are they? You need to figure out what is draining your energy and get those depletions in your life addressed. Here is a partial list of what I call Foundational Needs. See if these needs are covered adequately in your life.

Sleep

Food

Exercise

Housing

Beauty

Friendship

Connection

Appreciation

Financial security

Uncluttered house or office

Freedom from worry

Love

Respect

Lack of fears and phobias

Health

Spirituality or religious faith

Good relationship with family members

Go over this list again. Is something here draining your energy?[33] What are you tolerating that just exhausts you? If you can name 3 things that drain your energy, or 3 things you are tolerating that do not serve you, write those down and then write what you must do to get your needs met. For example, if you pick sleep, write down how many hours of sleep you need. If you picked appreciation, write down how you can receive other's appreciation more. If you picked exercise make a concrete plan to join a gym, go to yoga or zumba classes, or take a walk at least every other day.

You might be asking, "What does this have to do with forgiveness?" The answer is "everything." It's essential to learn to get your needs met and to be responsible for getting them met. All healthy relationships have clear and well established boundaries.

I want to say this again:

HEALTHY RELATIONSHIPS HAVE CLEAR AND WELL ESTABLISHED BOUNDARIES.

Boundaries help people to respect and appreciate each other. Honoring someone's boundaries is one of the most loving things you can do. It is what saves relationships. Knowing your own needs and expressing them is imperative. Knowing your partner's and family members' needs and boundaries and respecting them is fundamental – keeping the relationships safe and satisfying.

Maybe it is easy for you to just fall into co-dependent relationships. Maybe you have found yourself lost in other people from time to time, from relationship to relationship. Please enjoy this paragraph from *Eat, Pray, Love: One Woman's Search for Everything Across Italy, India and Indonesia* by Elizabeth Gilbert, (Penguin Books 2007)

> *Moreover, I have boundary issues with men. Or maybe that's not fair to say. To have issues with boundaries, one must have boundaries in the first place, right? But I disappear into the person I love. I am the permeable membrane. If I love you, you can have everything. You can have my time, my devotion, my ass, my money, my family, my dog, my dog's money, my dog's time – everything. If I love you, I will carry for you all your pain, I will assume for you all your debts (in every definition of the word), I will protect you from your own insecurity, I will project upon you all sorts of good qualities that you have never actually cultivated in yourself and I will buy Christmas presents for your entire family. I will give you the sun and the rain, and if they are not available, I will give you a sun check and a rain check. I will give you all this and more, until I get so exhausted and depleted that the only way I can recover my energy is by becoming infatuated with someone else.*

One of the biggest "ah-has" clients receive working with me is that we teach people how to treat us. If we get involved in a relationship and we give and give and we project that we are doormats with no needs or expectations, then we should not be surprised when we are treated that way. But people are often shocked when a year into a relationship they are still being treated the way they taught someone to treat them originally! Then they become martyrs. "I give and I give and get nothing in return!"

If it seems like you are constantly getting disappointed with your loved ones and you feel like you have to forgive all the time, a good inquiry is whether you have unreasonable expectations. Oftentimes those expectations create a lack or void in our lives. We are looking for someone else to fulfill us and then we are disappointed when they fail to meet our expectations or assumptions. It is truly better when we start taking responsibility for creating our own happiness and meeting our own needs and desires. Then our expectations become more realistic and our need for forgiveness is diminished.

Ask for what you need.
Teach people how to treat you.

Now, here is the hard part. What typically happens, especially for women, is that we do not ask for what we want or need and then we get mad when it is not given. We give and give and give and then we get exhausted. When we are exhausted from giving and not receiving, we become very unattractive martyrs. We feel taken advantage of, used, and unappreciated.

Once we are at the end of our rope, we get angry, we start spiraling downwards, and we start demanding what we need. It's ugly. I can see both men and women shaking their heads as you all know this scenario. Men, how frustrating is it for you when the woman you love will not receive your help to make their lives easier? Women, you know exactly what I am talking about. For those in same sex relationships, it doesn't matter what role you play, as long as you understand there are always roles you play vis–a-vis giving and receiving.

Knowing your needs and setting clear boundaries makes room for grace to come in and for forgiveness to flow.

How do you get your needs met with grace? Grace and compassion come easier when your needs are getting met on a regular basis. So, withdraw your membership from the "I can do it myself" club and start asking for and accepting help to get your needs met regularly. Once you accept and receive from others, you will feel less angry and less like a martyr. God gives us the grace we need to meet our challenges in life, and we need to be willing participants by accepting help from God and others in our lives.

Mirror Effect

Another tool I want to share with you when people in your life are driving you crazy is called the mirror effect. This also made a big difference in my relationship with my mother. At one time, she was constantly talking in a way that made it clear she was afraid that she would not have enough money. I mean it was non-stop; her fear and holding on tight to her money was driving me crazy. When something affects you in that way, when you are triggered like that, before you set boundaries, ask, how is that showing up in my life? Most likely, a shadow aspect of YOU is showing up in the person you want to push away. It is something you might consider ugly or embarrassing. Interestingly, this came up while I was visiting her about five years ago. I asked myself, where does this show up? I realized that I was worried about money and holding onto it also. On the outside I seemed generous and gave money away. However, on the inside, I was holding on tight. UGH! I was trying to stuff this aspect of myself in a deep dark place and did not want to look at it. Once I did, accepted this part of me, my mother's tightness with money didn't bother me. Miraculous!

Now I can say, thank you mom for teaching me to forgive this aspect in myself that I did not honor. Once I forgave myself, I was able to forgive her. Sometimes, it's the other way around, forgiving someone else can open room to forgive, accept and have more compassion for self.

So let's go back to Boundaries and Forgiveness.

I am now addressing those EXTREME cases where you are emotionally, verbally or physically abused and you need to protect yourself. You are sick and tired of being someone's physical or emotional punching bag. You have already told them that they can not treat you this way and they will not stop. You have already looked at your situation and taken personal responsibility for your part in the relationship. You've tried to change yourself by becoming more accepting and understanding and it hasn't worked. You have already prayed for a miracle to happen, to open the person's heart, and to change the unwanted behavior.

This is when you need to make a huge decision, and stop allowing this person to interfere in your life. How do you do this when it's a parent, a brother or sister, an in-law, or a cousin? What if it is your child who keeps showing up and taking advantage of you or is harming other family members?

> **If you continue to live in an abusive situation, you are still a victim.**
>
> **If you are still a victim, you are blaming someone else for your situation.**
>
> **You cannot blame and forgive at the same time.**
>
> **Releasing blame empowers you to find peace and move on with your life.**

If you continue to live in abuse, and be a victim, you can't really forgive. There is a difference between acknowledging what happened and living like a victim.[34] Once you are away from the abuser, you can forgive and let go. They no longer control you.

I recognize there are people who in the middle of being violated by rape are able to pray for their rapist. There are people who, like Nelson Mandela, are suffering at the hands of their offenders and still forgive. There was a man who was shot in a Colorado movie theatre recently and forgave the man and prayed for him immediately. I am in awe of people like this. I wish we could all be like that. However, this book is written to help the person who is still struggling with forgiveness and has not yet reached that level of enlightenment.

I can tell you, however, that everyone can make the decision to cut people out of their lives who are abusive and hurting them. The hardest part of this is making a decision and enforcing it. You might want to give the person a clear warning that if the behavior does not change, the relationship will end. Please do not give a warning unless you can abide by it. Once someone like this is out of your life, you are safe, and you can breathe, then you can forgive.

Litmus test: If you try and try and try to forgive, but you still feel hurt, angry, or bitter, then that is a sign that a boundary may need to be set.

Be honest with yourself. Are you unable to forgive because someone continues to abuse or re-offend you? Are you blaming yourself because you feel like you are supposed to forgive but cannot?

Even Master Saint Germain, a great advocate of forgiveness, reminds us that sometimes the thing we really need is to create boundaries. If you did not read the introduction to this book, please go back and read his channeling right now. Boundaries are the glue that holds relationships together. Create strong clear ones, and relationships can flourish. Dealing with people with certain mental health problems, addictions, crazy or abusive behavior, just might call for the boundary of no longer being in your life or at least limiting your exposure to them. If you have to make this decision for your own physical or emotional well-being, I support you and honor this difficult path you must take.

~~~***~~~
~~~

Section 3

Living with Forgiveness

Chapter 10

Building Your Forgiveness Muscle

Forgiveness Processes

> *"Holding on to anger, resentment and hurt only gives you tense muscles, a headache and a sore jaw from clenching your teeth. Forgiveness gives you back the laughter and the lightness in your life."*
>
> *~ Joan Lunden*

Forgiveness is different for everyone. There is no "right" way to forgive. With that being said, I am glad to share with you what has worked for so many of my clients. For some people, they can just go into their hearts and think or feel, "I forgive you" and for others, they need a multi-dimensional approach. That was me. For years I taught a 26 step process, which included affirmations, writing, finishing sentences, the Emotional Freedom Technique, the Sedona Method, journaling, and visualizations. I figured if I threw everything into the pot, certainly something would stick! My left brain was very active and needed to be fully engaged. I know, it sounds sort of crazy, but honestly it made a lot of sense to me at the time, because my own forgiveness path was so convoluted. The layers of the onion just went on forever! So, I will share with you everything that spirit wants me to share with you, and I have faith that something I write here will open your heart and speak to your soul.

Here you will find a number of options: meditations, affirmations, visualizations and journaling questions. I even included a healing based on EFT for those of you who love tapping, and a lesson using archetypes. The processes that follow are:

1. *Living with Forgiveness Process* you can use any time.
2. Healing the inner child with self love.
3. A journaling exercise to heal you when you've been hurt by your loved one.
4. A 7 step relationship healing using archetypes.
5. A very spiritual divorce/break-up healing journaling process.
6. An EFT process you can use and modify for any forgiveness issue.
7. A spiritual I AM affirmation process inspired by Saint Germain.

At the end of this chapter, I also include some additional bonuses: Daily Morning Routine I use to stay in alignment throughout the day, as well as a Weekly Manifesting Process I use with a girlfriend. I've included these so you can develop a routine that works for you. Feel free to use what makes sense to you.

I suggest skimming the processes below and see which ones attract you and do those. Trust your instincts with this.

~~~***~~~

Living with Forgiveness Visualization[35]

Take a deep 5 second breath in through your nose, and then slowly release it for another 5 seconds. Please do this again, 5 seconds in, 5 seconds out. Now, imagine you shrink and become a little person and you go into a little elevator located on the left side of your brain. See and push the heart button on the elevator and feel it slowly moving down your head, neck, upper chest down into your heart center. You have arrived at your heart center. The elevator doors open and you walk out into a beautiful light and you feel love surrounding you. You realize you are in touch, right this minute, with your higher self, your spirit.[36] Take some time to feel what it feels like to be this connected. Know all answers can come easily to you from this place.

Now, remember a time when someone hurt you. Acknowledge and accept what they did. Say the truth, tell the reality of the story to them and see them agreeing with you and understanding what you are saying/feeling. If they do not agree, be open to hear their side and come to a compromised agreement that you feel good with. What is the TRUTH of the situation? Accept the reality.

What was YOUR part in this situation? Past, present or future. Take personal responsibility for what is yours. Did you respond poorly? Where did you miss the mark in this relationship? Is there anything else you want to say to be complete?
~~~

What lessons did you learn? What did you learn about yourself, about how you respond in these situations? Are there some boundaries you need to develop? How could you be an even better person in relationships with others? Are there some changes you choose to make? What kind of growth did you experience from this situation?

Now, see that person in front of you and say and FEEL "Thank YOU!" Take another deep breath, place your hands on your heart, and feel thank you again. Feel gratitude for the lessons and the growth. This is what Forgiveness feels like. This is Living with Forgiveness.

You can slowly open your eyes with the next deep breath. Keep this feeling of forgiveness and love and gratitude with you all day.

~~~***~~~

Inner Child/Self Love

Because my feeling is that self-love through forgiveness ultimately goes back to forgiving ourselves for what we "perceive" are our inadequacies, I am going to share a visual-meditation you can do yourself. You can record the following message on a recording device, and then listen to it:

Close your eyes and take a deep breath in. Hold it for 5 seconds, and slowly release it for 5 seconds. Now, do that again: a 5 second breath in and a 5 second breath out. Allow your shoulders to relax with the
~~~

out-breath. Imagine going deep into your heart, and feel yourself there. You are now connected with everything you need to feel unconditional love for yourself. Stay there. Feel the stillness.

Now, picture yourself as a child, a small child, filled with innocence. You, your higher self, is going to have a conversation with the sweet, innocent part of you, the inner child that feels unloved and unappreciated. Now, allow that small child to tell you how they feel rejected by you, how you judge him/her. They might say something to you like, "I don't like it when you think I'm too fat" or "Every time you think the thought, "I'm stupid," it really hurts my feelings!" It could even be one of those so called unforgivable things like, "You keep blaming me for our son's death. It is not fair to keep blaming me!" Feel the pain it causes your inner child, your inner self, to be so judgmental. Now, I want you to take this precious child and hold him/her. See his/her innocence. Give this child all the love you can. Apologize for all the hurt you've caused over the years, all the self abuse, self-hatred, hurtful thoughts. Allow the child to speak to you as long as he/she wishes. Feel all the pain the child feels. Apologize again, from your heart. And with the loving innocence of a child, he/she will forgive you, completely. All the child ever wanted was to feel your love. Now it does. When you are complete, allow the child to merge back with you, into your heart space, clear and free from self-hate of any kind, no longer questioning your love.

Now, imagine God taking you both into his arms, hugging you, surrounding you, and telling you, "I love you my child, I created you, and I promise you that I make no mistakes. Not one part of you is a mistake.

You are perfect. I love you fully, and completely. I adore you and I want you to know, I have never left your side. Remember, as I am, so are you, for we are one. We are one. We are one."

~~~***~~~

When Someone You Love Hurts You Deeply (for a spouse-partner-love interest)

Close your eyes and take a deep breath in. Hold it for 5 seconds, and slowly release it for 5 seconds. Now, do that again: a 5 second breath in and a 5 second breath out. Imagine going deep into your heart, and feel yourself there. You are now connected with everything you need to feel unconditional love for yourself. Stay there. Feel the stillness.

Picture the person who hurt you in front of you. Don't move one inch until you clearly see them. Open your heart to this person. Allow yourself to feel vulnerable. You cannot be hurt. You are safe. It's okay to let your walls down.

Tell this person: "Once upon a time, we were in love. We were part of a soul group together, and we felt no pain, only love. We planned on coming to earth together, to support each other, just like we've done many times before. You were not only my lover, but my best friend. I trusted you completely."

"I understand that you love me so dearly and completely that you came to earth to support me in my personal growth. I wanted to learn
~~~

__________________. You agreed to help me by being or doing __________________________. To agree to be the bad one, the one to be blamed, you must love me deeply. I know that now and I forgive you."

"I am also mad at myself, because I _________ __________. (Note this is where you take responsibility for your part.) I realize that I am also blaming myself for ________________________. I am forgiving myself as I speak to you. Thank you for bringing this up for me so I can release and let go of the anger I carry towards myself. The truth is, a piece of me feels like a fool. I also carry shame and guilt that I need to release. Forgiving you is teaching me to forgive myself. I thank you for that."

"I am grateful for our coming together. I wanted to learn to _____________ and I did. This was a powerful and difficult lesson and the truth is, you were willing to come forth and help me learn it. Realizing this, I can no longer stay mad at you. I forgive you and thank you at the same time. I hope you can also forgive me for __________________ (be specific).

If there is anything else you'd like to say, this is the time and place to say it. If there is a response, allow it to come through. Be still and listen.

Now, remembering we are all one in spirit, allow yourselves to merge gently together. Feel the oneness. Feel the gentle flow of love between the two of you come together. Judgment leaves. Hurt washes away. Resentment and bitterness are in the past. Take a deep breath in and when you release it, feel the space that was once filled with hurt and anger. Feel the void and fill it with love and gratitude. Imagine it filling up with acceptance and spiritual understanding.

~~~***~~~

Lori's 7 Relationship Forgiveness Steps through Archetypes

If you like journaling and feel like playing around with using archetypes as a tool to heal, I want to share with you a good way to do that. Carl Jung on Archetypes by Pearson-Marr describes archetypes as follows: "Archetypes are psychological structures reflected in symbols, images, and themes common to all culture and all times. You see them in recurring images in art, literature, myths, and dreams. You may experience archetypes directly as different parts of you. If you say on one hand that you want one thing and on the other you want something else, you can give archetypal names to those parts, as they generally communicate desires and motivations common to humans everywhere. For example, while the Warrior is an archetype, different types of warriors engage in different battles. The Warrior archetype encompasses the Japanese Samurai and the American G.I., but it also might include the HIV researcher, the advocate for social justice, or the member of a street gang. Archetypes teach us that we have different aspects of ourselves and that wisdom can come from all those aspects."

Why do we use archetypes? Archetypes help us to get out of our heads, to hear our inner wisdom. It is easy
~~~

for us to say, "I don't know" or to look at every problem from the same perspective, our perspective. However, there is an incredible amount of power in looking at a problem and having instant access to how a warrior would handle it, how a king would handle it, and how a horse-whisperer would handle it for example.

Please note there could be hundreds of archetypes. Here are a few that all people possess:

> **Warrior** – action, strength, integrity, loyalty, courageousness, fearlessness.
>
> **Magician** – intuitive, knows it's all easy and instantly understands how absurd everything is, tricky, mystical, empowering.
>
> **Lover** – deepest emotions of love and connection, life vibrates from within heart, passion, beauty, romance, intimacy, sensual.
>
> **Sovereign** – clarity, what you are here to do, knows your vision and purpose, governs our lives, ruler, power, dependable, wise.

And women have the following archetypes:

> **Maiden** – innocence, curiosity, play, and creativity. The color is white, the color of purity and innocence.
>
> **Mother** – nurturer, life giver, empathetic, sympathetic, protector, warrior, nest-builder. The color is red, the color of menstrual blood.
>
> **Crone** – life experience, wise woman, healing, teaching, guiding. The color is black, the color of night.

If you have an archetype deck of cards, like the one from Carolyn Myss, pick one card from the deck. If you do not have a deck, pick one from the list above. If you are confused about the card you chose, look it up on the internet or pick another.

To really get into this exercise, you will make believe you are an actor and you are going to play a role. Ask and answer: "Where does the archetype reside in your body? Stand up. Feel the archetype. Stand how the archetypal person stands. Put your hand where the archetype resides in your body. What does it sound like? What kind of language does it use? What kind of thoughts does it have? Now, get ready, stand, feel, think, and speak like the archetype.

1. Say, "I invoke the archetype of the ________ ________________. Enter my body now!"

2. Then ask the following either in writing/journaling format, or using a recorder. If you have a partner who is willing to work with you on this process, ask for them to help you get in the role and have them ask you the questions. Then you answer from the voice of the archetype you chose. You might want to write down the questions you would like answers to, or use some from this list:

    Why was I in this relationship?

    What piece of this issue is mine?

    What personal responsibility do I have to take/ accept in this process?

    Can you stop blaming this person?

    How can you release the need to be right?

Why is it important for me to forgive ________________?

What lessons did I need to learn from this relationship?

From ________'s highest being, from his/her soul to yours, ask: what it is that ________ most loves and appreciates about me?

What did ____________ learn from me?

Why did my soul decide to come into this lifetime with __________________?

3. Take a deep breath and picture the person in front of you and say "I thank you and bless you for being willing to play a part in my healing. I honor myself for being willing to play a part in your healing." As you see the person in your mind's eye, say: "We are not enemies, but loving healing angels for one another."

4. Write: "I release from my consciousness all feelings of ________________. Thank you for teaching me to forgive, love and accept myself exactly as I am."

5. Write: "I realize my "story" came from the place of the hurt, angry, unhealed victim. I see now that I can change this reality. The situation was perfect because ________________________________ (explain in detail)."

6. Say out loud:

> Even though I felt unforgiving in the past, I unconditionally love and accept myself, just the way I am.
>
> I trust this situation has unfolded perfectly.
>
> I trust that I am reconnected with my source, my true nature, which is love.
>
> I feel love flowing into my life."

7. Coming from the place of your archetype, summarize and state your new story, including why you came together, what you each learned, and how lucky you are to have come together to share these experiences. Really accept the lessons and the gifts and feel the gratitude that comes from such acceptance.

~~~***~~~

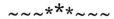

Lori's Forgiveness Process for Divorce or any Break-Up

Get ready for a miracle. This is a process I teach in my book, *Transcending Divorce: A Guide to Personal Growth and Transformation.* It is one that creates miracles. I've seen lawsuits settle and peace develop between family members who were once embattled in hatred and hurt. This is a very deep personal process and I believe the releases created through this
~~~

process allow things to heal on a spiritual level that we could never create on our own.

To do this process, allow yourself quiet time. Get into a meditative state. Give yourself at least 30 minutes for each question.

1. Write down what happened as if you were experiencing it all over again. Allow yourself to feel the anger, rage, disappointment and confusion. What expectations were crushed? Write out all the feelings involved. Notice if these feelings were similar to a time in your childhood where you may have felt the same. I noticed that my husband's cheating gave me the same feelings of rejection, abandonment, and 'not good enough' that I had after my father and mother divorced when I was 4. That is why the pain was so deep. It triggered me back to unhealed childhood feelings/memories.

2. Put yourself in your ex-spouse's shoes and write down what happened from his perspective. What feelings did he feel? What expectations of his were crushed?

3. Write down the "facts" as agreed upon by the two of you as you wrote above. These are the similarities of your stories. Maybe these facts are a little closer to the "truth" of the marriage. While you do this, you can also choose a few other perspectives for how you can view your marriage and its break-up. Don't forget to take responsibility for your own piece of the story. (Hint: Imagine that you were a spiritual being, planning to have a human experience in this

lifetime, and you were talking to a soulmate, someone you loved, and there was a particular lesson you wanted to learn. You asked him/her to come onto the earth plane, as a human being, and plan to meet at some point and get married. What would you ask him to do so that you could really learn the lesson you wished to learn?)

4. Before you do the following exercise, you really need to set aside **2 hours** of uninterrupted time. When you read your answer, you will probably feel teary, get chills up and down your spine, feel an overwhelming sense of peace, or something similar if you really get in that sacred space. If you do not feel a major feeling of recognition, then you probably need to wait a week or so and do it again. I am giving you an example of the letter I wrote, so you have an understanding of how deep this gets. I still am moved when I read my own letter, even 15+ years after my divorce! Expect miracles. These come with real forgiveness!

Higher-Self perspective exercise: This should take quite a while, so find a quiet place where you will not be disturbed. Get very still and quiet, breathe in and out slowly a few times. Ask God, Spirit, your guides, whatever/whomever you pray to, to help you with this. Now, image that you are your ex-spouse's higher self. Merge with his/her soul. This is very different from the personality/ego self. Remember, you are speaking from the spirit world in this exercise. Ask this soul what she/he wants to say to your soul, to your higher self. Ask what she/he loves and appreciates most about you. Get a clear understanding of how they really feel about you on a soul level.

I was able to see the miracles my clients received from this exercise. So when I became embroiled in my own court battles with my ex-husband, I decided I should just try the forgiveness process that works for my clients. I mean, they had miracles, so maybe I would too. My higher perspective letter follows:

> *Dearest Lori,*
>
> *I became lost in this life, and hurting you was a by-product of my confusion. In fact, marrying each other was also a byproduct of my confusion. This isn't to say I didn't love you, for I certainly felt love and passion for you. It means that I had my head up my ass when I began cheating on Joanne – you have such good instincts and you let me talk you out of them. Your desire to have children was stronger than your inner guidance system. Go back and read your journal, you'll see what I mean.*
>
> *I always respected you and wanted your respect back. I couldn't help feel that I was always letting you down, from the very beginning, when I had no money and you had to pay for us to go and come back from Israel, giving up your dream for me . . . . I felt like a fuck-up right from the beginning. Leaving my kids, not being wanted on the kibbutz, choosing to return to the states, I saw how you were giving and giving and I was floundering.*

I got hit by the car in Harrisburg to slow me down so I had some time to think about what to do next. I was just in a panic mode at that point.

I tried to impress you with my intelligence and used my broad knowledge base to accomplish that. You loved that part of me; I felt it and reveled in your pride in me at those times. That is how I was able to get the job at the JCC – I felt good about that part of myself.

I know you have asked the question over the years, was any part of our marriage real? Do you remember reading the book, "What to expect when you are expecting?" Remember trying to get pregnant and wanting to get pregnant? All of that was real . . . I just want you to know.

Oh, you gave me the best. Our son was all I wasn't. I had such hopes he would be a better man than me and you know what Lori, he will be. I was also jealous of him – it was clear to me he became your first love. It wasn't just the diminishing sex, it was the look in your eye, you were so consumed with him and there was no room left for me. I imagined it would be me taking care of him, like I did with Joanne. But your instincts kicked in and you were in charge.

Then you were in charge of everything. Of course, we even had our house because of your family. It was you who got us out of that apartment.

When years later I told you that I think our lack of sexual intimacy was my age, you got on the Internet and did research, tried everything you could to help me find out what was wrong. Again, you believed my lies. This was my way to control you, as I felt so controlled. It became sort of a mantra for me, and a way to escape what I saw as an unhappy marriage. I know it looked like a perfect marriage to you, that's because I met all your needs. I am very good at being adaptable, as you are well aware.

I took pride in how I had this secret life – it could have gone on forever! I could fantasize about this whole other world and still be this respectable husband and father. Hah!

I never thought of the consequences, because I was so smart, I knew I would never get caught. Of course, eventually, the money got out of hand and that's where I lost it.

You were right to divorce me right away; I kept lying to you even after we were divorced, trying to get back together. I'm a great actor Lori, you never realized – this life is just a play and I had a starring role in your life.

I know you want to know where I am now. Frankly honey – that is none of your business. I am doing my own thing and you need to move forward and do yours. I know you have recognized the great gifts I keep giving you – the lawsuits, the doubting yourself, the worrying about the kids, the "gremlins" (as you call it) in your mind and all that spiritual and personal growth stuff for which your soul longs. You are so much more peaceful than I ever knew. I have become angry and bitter in my dealings with you, perhaps it is because I see how happy you are and how you have moved on.

Now go forward, keep doing the terrific job you've been doing raising our children. They are great kids – our daughter is so like you – I am afraid she feels it when I look at her and see you – I do love her, but as you know, I really do come first in this lifetime. We'll have our own paths together and we will learn and grow from each other – you can be sure of that!

You always complimented me as a teacher. You are right, I'm a great teacher. But Lori, so are you! You are a great teacher for me, for the kids, for all those people whose life you touch with your work. I know you never realized this inside yourself and I'm glad you are awakening to it now.

So Lori, keep love in your heart, I'll feel it even when I'm not there. It will soften me eventually, as will time, and we can then finish our little dance.

(Note: This was written on January 2. On January 7 I got a friendly e-mail that he wanted to settle our outstanding legal cases. (He even mentioned something about being too old to fight and this not 'spiritually' serving him.) On January 14, our child support modification was settled and on January 18, the parenting time and support appeal was settled.

This is the power of loving thoughts and forgiveness from a spiritual level.)

There are two more steps you can take if you feel like it:

> - Write a thank-you note to yourself for all the gifts and lessons learned, and for finding the courage to be brave and trusting.
>
> - Write a thank-you note to your spouse for all the gifts and lessons.

~~~***~~~

Emotional Freedom Technique (EFT)[37] With Thanks to Gary Craig, Carol Look and Roberta Roth

This technique brings relief for many physical and emotional problems related to forgiveness. Exceptions generally occur when one gives up too soon or becomes apathetic. This does not work for everyone, but the people it does work for just swear by it. This is a simplified and limited version of what you might receive when you work with an EFT licensed practitioner.

It works by tapping on certain meridian points in the body, and allows the energy of the belief system to flow through and out of the body. Basically, it allows beliefs or negative thoughts to become un-stuck.
~~~

If this is new for you, you might want to google EFT or go to **www.CarolLook.com** to see how this procedure is done.

EFT SET-UP: First ask yourself: "What is the issue or problem?" Write it down.

Next ask, "How bad is it?" Tune into the body feelings and measure them on a scale of 0 to 10, with 10 being the most intense.

We are going to use the example of feeling hurt and angry because someone has hurt you. You can get very specific in your feelings.

E.F.T. ALGORITHM:

A. Repeat the following as you tap "karate chop point" on the side of your hands, pinky sides in: "Even though I am so hurt and angry because . . . (this problem), I deeply and completely love and accept myself, and God loves me."

Example: Even though I don't think this tapping will help me, and even though I am furious with my daughter, or grieving my friend's death, or have knee pain, I deeply and completely love and accept myself, and I choose to let go of . . . . (Note: add in as many aspects of the issue as come to mind when you're doing this. For example, if it is about something you did, you might say "Even though I am so embarrassed I did . . .," or "Even though I am so mad at myself for . . ." If someone else hurt you, you might repeat, "Even though I feel like a fool for allowing . . . to hurt me again," or "Even though I want to forgive . . . I am still so angry and hurt.")

B. Now tap or rub the following points on face and upper body, a number of times in each place, while you say the words and thought patterns. As you do this, just name the problem at each point. E.g., "back pain," "outrage," "guilt," "anger at ______________," "fear of ______________," or "confusion."

1. Between Eyebrows (4 fingers)
2. Outside Eyes (on temples)
3. Under Eyes (on bone)
4. Under Nose above Lip
5. Under Lip (on chin)
6. Collarbone (under bones)
7. Under Arm (4″ down from armpits)
8. Top of Head

C. Now measure how strongly you feel the feelings again and write it down. If it is not at 1 or 0, do another round of EFT, saying at point A, "Even though I <u>still</u> have this problem, I deeply and completely love and accept myself and God loves me (3x)."

D. Repeat the whole process again. Then as you tap on face/upper body and fingers/hand, simply say the phrase, "still hurt," or "still hate . . ." or "remaining back pain" or "remaining anger," etc.

E. Continue new rounds of EFT until you bring the measurement to a 1 or a 0.

F. I then use the last round to be very positive and upbeat. "I am a forgiving person. I easily forgive. I release anger quickly. I learn my lessons with ease and grace. I appreciate all the gifts . . . brings into my life. I love myself and God loves me . . . ." Say whatever resonates with you.

At the end, take a few deep breaths and allow the energy to flow before you stand up.

~~~***~~~

Forgiveness "I AM" Decrees, written with guidance from Saint Germain

Feel free to say these out loud whenever you are moved to do so. There is great energy with whatever we say after the words "I AM!" That is why it is so important to watch our language and not put ourselves down. Speak these positive affirmations until you feel them.

I AM that I AM

I AM the Christ on earth

I AM the embodiment of compassion

I AM all that I AM

I AM one with the creator

I AM one with my higher self, my soul

I AM the forgiver and

I AM the forgiven

I AM all that I AM
~~~

I AM of the light
I AM the one Love
I AM oneness
I AM the one who hurts as
I AM the one who is hurt
I AM as I judge and
I AM the judged
I AM all that I AM and
I AM ONE
I AM perfect in my flaws
I AM loved as flawless
I AM free from my mind
I AM beautiful and wise
I AM grace and wisdom
I AM empowered and
I AM brave
I AM courageous and
I AM strong
I AM able to face the truth
That I AM all that I AM and
I AM ONE with God.
I AM ONE with All.
Amen, Amen, Amen
And so it is!

~~~***~~~

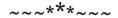

BONUSES:
Daily Morning Practice

Here is a 10 minute morning practice that will help you stay on track with forgiveness, self-love and acceptance. It is a great way to develop compassion and live from your heart. You can even stay in bed to do this. I do this regularly and you can do it too. If you forget, the world will not end and if you want to modify it in any way, please do so. This is all about what works for you.

When you awaken, go right into your heart space – literally breathe into your heart. This will remind you immediately to live from this place today. You can put your hand on your heart if it helps.

Next, breathe through all your chakras, and then breathe from your toes out the top of your head and back down again. This will energize your body in a gentle way. If you need to stretch, feel free to do that too, even before getting out of bed.

Do your "I am" mantras: "I AM healthy, wealthy, beautiful and wise." (I used to wake up and my "to do" list was running, or a complaint about how I didn't get enough sleep, "I'm sore," or "oh sh*t I have to get going and it's raining/cold" etc.)

Now, I am healthy, wealthy, beautiful and wise just pops into my head.
~~~

Do your "I AM grateful for . . ." and list 5 things. We can say 5 things, or we can feel 5 things. Feeling 5 things is more powerful. Throughout the Living with Forgiveness processes, we spoke about gratitude. It is easy to do and if you really don't have something to feel grateful for, then feel gratitude for where you imagine you are going, your future self, who is also healthy, wealthy, beautiful and wise. As I was writing this book, I was grateful for all the readers and the difference it was making in their lives.

If you have anything you need help with for the day, ask your angels and guides to help you make it happen, with ease and grace.

Surround yourself with golden white light, Christ Consciousness Light, like a bubble, protecting you. Ask it to only allow love and light inside. Your aura is now protected.

Ask if there is any karma you took on, any anger or hurt you feel, or you caused another. If yes, ask for it to be released now. If you did something you are not proud of yesterday, forgive yourself and assure yourself that you will do better today. Include even simple things like, "I was really pissed off at the guy in front of me driving 9 mph in a 35 mph zone." Acknowledge that and release it. There is absolutely no reason to take on anger from yesterday into today. Let it go.

If you have a prayer to say, say it, see it, feel it.

And finally, go back from where you started, your heart space, and set an intention for the day. It can be about money, it can be about staying in your heart space, it can be about world peace or about not yelling at your mother or teenager, about your work with clients or even something like, "Let me be on time for all my appointments."

End with a thank you to the universe, God, your guides or yourself. Thank you is a powerful prayer.

As you have time, you can add a 10–20 minute quiet meditation to your routine.

~~~***~~~

"Act as If" or "Perfect Life" Discussion

My friend Lisa shared this idea with me and I've been doing it for over a year. On a weekly basis, I talk to my friend Veeanna by phone about our perfect life, as if we are living our perfect lives. We each share for about 10 minutes. We get excited for each other, we even shed tears of joy when we hear how great we are doing. We literally bring our dreams, our goals to life right now. We hold the energy for each other to be big, to live big, right now.

A conversation might sound like this: "I found the perfect car that I always wanted! It's a red GTI, very sporty and very fast! It's adorable and we were able to afford it without any problem! I love it!" And the response will be something like: "Oh My Gosh, that is great! I am so excited for you! Send me a picture of it!" "OK, I will as soon as we get off the phone!" Can you see the energy behind that?
~~~

In the last year, we both ended up with new vehicles, Veeanna bought a condo that she never thought she could afford, and went on a dream scuba-diving trip to Fiji and I lost the 30 pounds I never thought I could release. For us, staying positive, in gratitude for what we have, feeling the vibration of having/doing/being all that we can be, is working. I hope you will find a friend to do this perfect life exercise with.

~~~***~~~

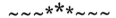

As you can see, there is NO right way or wrong way to forgive, to meditate, to release. I gave you so many different kinds of processes so that you can pick and choose which ones work best for you. This is not a book that tells you that you must do A, B, and C in order to forgive. This book is about choices, ideas, and learning what resonates with you and what does not.

If you have developed a great forgiveness process that works for you and you want to share it with others, please write to me and let's see if we can get it up into my blog on www.Lori Rubenstein.com.

~~~***~~~

Chapter 11

Conclusion

The Journey Back to Love

"I hope you never lose your sense
of wonder
You get your fill to eat
But always keep that hunger
May you never take one single breath
forgranted
God forbid love ever leave you
empty handed
I hope you still feel small
When you stand beside the ocean
Whenever one door closes,
I hope one more opens
Promise me that you'll give fate
a fighting chance
And when you get the choice to
sit it out or dance
I hope you dance
I hope you dance . . . ."

From the Song, "I Hope You Dance"
by Lee Ann Womack

Forgiveness is all about the journey back to love. What if we woke up tomorrow and remembered who we really are? What would we discover? Perhaps we would know that everything is perfect as it is, that we are perfect as we are. Perhaps we would know that we came on this journey to experience something we can not experience as spirit – the re-discovery of love. As spiritual beings without the human form, we cannot experience discovering love, because we already know that is what we are. There is no duality.

The gift of human existence is in the discovery, in the journey we take to find ourselves. And this journey is a courageous one!

I want to share this poem by Peter Rengel,[38] from his book *Living Life in Love*, because it is basically the entire premise of this book.

Forgiveness

Feeling forgiveness is
A beautiful release from
The prison of the past.
But, the very need to forgive
Shows that you have judged.
Let go of all judgments
And you will never need
To forgive anyone again.

But here is the irony: we must accept that we will continue to judge again and then forgive when we do judge, because we will judge! Accept that this is true. Don't try to fight it or argue it away. I know it is lofty to reach for the stars and say that we know that the truth is that there is nothing to forgive. However, we are still human and this is our courageous journey back to love!

So it is time for all of us to imagine a world of peace, the peace that starts with each of us individually doing our respective parts in creating it. It is our responsibility to step into this new golden age, to act as though we believe that our thoughts and actions actually do affect how the world responds.

While the world is at a choice point, we too are at a critical and personal choice point. Do we choose to live in the past and walk around with a chip on our shoulders and blame our unhappiness on the past, playing the part of the victim, or do we choose to accept that obstacles and challenges are part of our path and be grateful for our soul's lessons and growth?

Never let your past experiences destroy your future.

Your past can't be altered.

It's time to stop punishing yourself and choose to embrace a joyful future.

I wrote this book so you don't have to spend years angry or holding on to grudges like I did. It's easy to get stuck in an obsessive pattern of trying to understand and figure out the past. When we do this, we are trying in some way to change the past, to rewrite the story. As a seeker, it's important to remember that what you really want is to be happy now and to manifest a new, happier, healthier future.

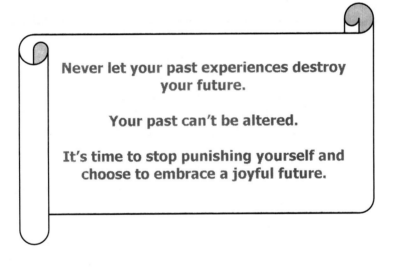

We must start by setting our focus and our intentions on where we want to be in the future, and then ask the question, how do I get there? What is the next step? If we spend all our time analyzing the past and if our thoughts are in the past, doesn't it follow that our future is going to match the feelings-emotions-beliefs of our past?

You cannot drive the car forward looking in the rear-view mirror.

I hope you make the choice to live now and in each moment of future nows, recognizing that each choice we make today takes us on a particular path. From a spiritual perspective, there is no right or wrong path, all are lessons. From a human perspective, some paths are easier than others. I'd like to learn lessons in a more gentle way rather than bang my head against a wall.

I share with you one of the first lessons I learned in coaching school: **"The Past Does Not Equal the Future."** It's a good thing too. If that were not the case, intergenerational abuse would never end, there would be no hope of ending alcoholism or drug addiction, and the Earth would have no hope of peace.

Everything must come to an end. A door must close in order for a new one to open. My past has taught me that the closing doors may seem scary at first, but if we keep walking through the door, we will see the blessings revealed. You might just have to go through the pain to get to the other side. If you work hard to avoid and stuff the pain, you might never be gifted the beautiful life awaiting you on the other side. When I became aware of this, my new mantra became: **"This too shall pass."** It honestly has gotten me through all my difficult times in the last decade of my life. If we spend all our time focused on our fears, on that closed door, we leave no room for the new one to open. Moreover, if a door does open, we won't even notice the new one because all our attention is focused on the closed door.

It is my honor to be your guide in this forgiveness book, and I hope you have had those sensations of what it feels like to let go, to release, to feel freedom from the past, from your judgments, from all the "should haves" of your life. As you step into this new chapter in your life, may you be blessed with love, with the remembrance of the beautiful soul you really are, and with the gift of peace that comes with regular forgiveness.

~~~***~~~
~~~

I leave you with one of my favorite poems:

The Prayer of St. Francis

Lord, make me an instrument
of your peace,
Where there is hatred,
let me sow love;
where there is injury, pardon;
where there is doubt, faith;
where there is despair, hope;
where there is darkness, light;
where there is sadness, joy;

O Divine Master, grant that I may not so much
seek to be consoled as to console;
to be understood as to understand;
to be loved as to love.
For it is in giving that we receive;
it is in pardoning that we are pardoned;
and it is in dying that we are
born to eternal life.

End Notes

[1] Author Gregg Braden says a choice point is the time between the ending of one cycle and the beginning of the next. He claims that this is the final 5,125 year cycle in a 26,000 year cycle and that there is massive potential to choose the future, right now. 2012 is the choice point.

[2] For more information see *Spiritual Psychology: The Twelve Primary Life Lessons* by Steve Rother (2004)

[3] In Judaism, on Yom Kippur, the Day of Atonement, forgiveness is requested. We even say to someone, if there is anything I've done to you in the past year that has hurt you, please forgive me. If we ask someone to forgive us three times and they refuse, it is said that we are forgiven anyway. I had hurt someone very much when we broke up. I asked for forgiveness for years and since I never got that kind of acknowledgment, I took the route of "I'm officially forgiven." And, I had to forgive myself for causing the pain.

[4] I do recognize that you might not share the same fundamental beliefs as I do. The goal here is to be accepting and flexible. Use what makes sense to you and what works for you. Use your own internal guidance system.

[5] There are other spiritual practices that bring people closer to spirit, such as meditation, walking in nature, reading, yoga, studying religious texts, praying, A Course in Miracles, etc. Forgiveness is recognized as a fundamental principle in all spiritual practices.

[6] The body responds to thoughts and questions and by raising an arm and asking the person to hold it strong, you can get weak or strong responses. Many doctors are using

kinesiology to assist them in making their diagnoses of patients.

[7] Dr. Robert Young from Australia has been studying the effects of thoughts on our biology for 25 years. "Your mental state is so very critical. Your mental state, in many ways, if it's negative, can create more metabolic acids than the food that you're eating. In fact, you can create two or three times more metabolic acids from your thoughts and your mental state than from ingesting acidic foods, such as dairy or animal protein.

So your thoughts are critical. Your thoughts or words do become matter and can affect your physiology in a negative or positive way. And the way your thoughts become biology is as follows: when you have a thought, that thought requires energy for the brain cells to produce that thought. As you carry on with any thought that are having, you are using energy. And when you are using energy, you produce a biological waste product called, acid. If the metabolic acids from your thoughts are not properly eliminated through the four channels of elimination – urination, perspiration, respiration and defecation – then the acids from your thoughts are moved out into your fatty tissues and connective tissues. This leads to all sorts of symptomologies such as lupus, fibromyalgia, arthritis, muscle pain, fatigue, tiredness, obesity, cancerous breasts, cancerous prostate, indigestion, acid reflux, heart burn, heart attacks, and the list goes on and on."

[8] From the website, www.CancerfightingStrategies.com, it states, "Taking medicines or supplements for cancer while your pH is highly acidic is a bit like washing dishes in a sink

of dirty water, even when you put in plenty of soap, you can't get the dishes clean."

According to Keiichi Morishita in his book, *Hidden Truth of Cancer* (1972) "when your blood starts to become acidic, your body deposits acidic substances (usually toxins) into cells to allow the blood to remain slightly alkaline. This causes your cells to become more acidic and toxic, which results in a decrease of their oxygen levels, and harms their DNA and respiratory enzymes."

Over time, he theorizes, these cells increase in acidity and some die. These dead cells themselves turn into acids. However, *some* of these acidified cells may adapt in that environment. In other words, instead of dying – as normal cells do in an acid environment – some cells survive by becoming abnormal cells.

These abnormal cells are called malignant cells. Malignant cells do not correspond with brain function nor with our own DNA memory code. Therefore, malignant cells grow indefinitely and without order. This is cancer.

As you can see, he is describing, from a different point of view, the link between pH and cancer, a process by which low oxygen levels turn some cells cancerous. Alkaline water (including the water in cells) holds a lot of oxygen. Acidic water holds very little oxygen. So the more acidic your cells are, the less oxygenated they will be. To make matters worse, the fermentation process cancer cells use to produce energy creates lactic acid, further increasing acidity and reducing oxygen levels.

Sang Whang, in his book *Reverse Aging* (1991 and 2012 Kindle) points out that toxins are acidic. If your blood is too acidic, toxins will not be released from your cells into the blood. So your cells can't be detoxified. This buildup of toxins in your cells results in acidic, poorly oxygenated cells, which can turn cancerous. He explains, "In general, degenerative diseases are the result of acid waste buildups within us. When we are born, we have the highest alkaline mineral concentration and also the highest body pH. From that point on, the normal process of life is to gradually acidify. That is why these degenerative diseases do not occur when you are young. Reverse aging requires two separate steps: chemical and physical. The first step is to lower the acidity of the body so that it can dispose of acidic wastes in the blood and cellular fluids safely and easily. The second step is to physically pull out old stored wastes into the blood stream so that they can be discharged from the body."

As you learn about pH and cancer, you find there is a long history of reversing cancer by adding alkalinity to the body (along with your doctor's recommendations). It is one of the basic strategies in the battle against cancer and for improving your health in general.

[9] See *The Biology of Belief: Unleashing the Power of Consciousness, Matter, and Miracles,* by Bruce Lipton (Hay House, 2008).

[10] Author of *Breaking the Habit of Being Yourself: How to Lose Your Mind and Create a New One* (Hay House, 2012).

[11] *Transcending Divorce: A Guide to Personal Growth and Transformation,* (2nd edition 2011)

[12] Virginia Commonwealth University. The University of Maryland Institute of Human Virology discovered that forgiveness lowers the stress hormone cortisol and the immune system is boosted. Furthermore, Stanford University Center for Research in Disease Prevention said,

"When you hold onto the bitterness for years, it stops you from living your life fully. As it turns out, it wears out your immune system and hurts your heart."

[13] Although I know you understand I am an attorney turned mediator turned coach turned forgiveness teacher, and NOT a medical doctor, I need to put in the warning that I am NOT a doctor and am NOT giving you medical opinions or treatments for any diagnosis you may have received. Go to your doctor AND if you both agree, you can choose to incorporate the suggestions in this book.

[14] Patti Conklin, CEO and Founder of Healing Within, Inc. teaches that color and tone are active vibrations, which means that they have the frequency necessary to shake loose cellular memory from an individual cell. Her essay can be found in *Faces Behind the Pages that Inspire* (2012) and her new book, *God Within* coming out in 2012.

[15] Note from Author: In an over-simplified explanation, Ho'oponopono means to *make right* and is an ancient Hawaiian practice of reconciliation and forgiveness. Basically, you acknowledge the creator by saying "I am sorry," describe what happened, ask for forgiveness, and say "I love you." Fill that person up with love, and say or feel "I thank you." If someone has hurt you, you can do this for yourself and them, as it is believed we are all one. If you forgive someone, you are both forgiven.

[16] In all my years working as a legal advocate or attorney for abuse survivors, the number one reason people gave for not leaving abusive relationships was fear of losing children. Since the abusers were omnipotent to the victims, this threat, to take the children, works to keep abused spouses prisoners in their own lives.

[17] http://www.terrinewlon.com/Bardo.php

[18] Michael says there are seven soul types and gives guidelines for understanding your type. Basically, Michael says we are one of the following: Kings, Priests, Sages, Scholars, Warriors, Artisans, or Servers. It's hard to tell from the names what you are, you'll need to read the book for the descriptions and questions/guidelines.

[19] Akashic Records, aka the Hall of Records, is the place where all the stories and lifetimes here on Earth are stored. As the veil becomes thinner, more and more people are accessing the Akashic Records. Christine Laureano is one of them.

[20] If you feel like tossing this book against the wall right now, that's okay. Toss the book and then pick it up again. You might certainly have a different spiritual belief. That is fine. Keep reading and I will give you something you can use to work through this process. We are in this together and all I want to do is help you to forgive so you can be happy again.

[21]13 year old author of *Anne Frank: The Diary of a Young Girl* written while she was hiding in a secret annex in Holland before she was discovered and taken to Auschwitz and perished at age 15.

[22] Author of *Soul Centered: Transform Your Life in 8 Weeks with Meditation* (Hay House 2009)

[23] Holding on to guilt, shame, and self-blame serves nothing and no one and it is a useless, time-wasting behavior.

[24] As a child, shame can be brought about by alienation, abandonment, rejection, physical, verbal and emotional abuse. The child learns to believe that there is something inherently wrong with him/her.

[25] NY Times best selling author of *Healing the Shame that Bind's You* (Revised HCI, 2005)

[26] I will use 'He' and sometimes I will use 'She' to describe God. I do not believe God is one or the other, but who knows?

[27] The full realization of your potential. In human terms, we might look at an ascended master as someone who is actualized. For example, even though Jeshua (Jesus) was in earth body, he knew of his own gifts, who he really was, a soul having a human experience, with the ability to heal and help others through the belief and faith that he is one with God.

[28] To find a soul regression therapist near you: http://www.iblrn.org. To read more about soul regressions, I recommend reading *Journey of Souls* or *Destiny of Souls* by Dr. Michael Newton, *Bringing Your Soul to Light* by Dr. Linda Backman, or *Many Lives, Many Masters* by Dr. Brian Weiss.

[29] Karma can look like a payback, a "what goes around comes around." However, it is not actually a punishment; it is more of an evening out. For our soul's progression, we want things to be fairer. We want to know both sides of all experiences. A good way to look at karma is that it is a natural consequence of our actions, or harvesting what we sow. Religious sects have varying views on karma. It is my

belief that regular forgiveness and acceptance helps us to release karmic ties and move our lessons forward.

[30] Peter Rengel is a spiritual counselor living in California, whose poetry has touched my heart for many years. His website is www.PeterRengel.com.

[31] If we are all God's children, then why would She take sides? We humans are irrational and illogical if we think that in a "war environment" that God would protect one side against another.

[32] Some people also have ascended master guides such as Jeshua, Mary, Gandhi, Saint Germain, Krishna, Buddha, Djwahl-Kuhl, Maitreya, Quan Yin, and some have the Archangels. We have guides who have served on earth, some with us in previous incarnations, and some who have never been on earth. We also, interestingly, have guides who have specialties. For example, if you are an artist, you very well could have Rembrandt or Botticelli as one of your master guides. I know that when I was an attorney, I had a brilliant Native American Chief who helped me speak in court. Some guides are with you a life-time, others for a shorter period of time. You probably know someone who has told you a miraculous story of how they were saved from death and they do not know how it was possible, yet they feel unable to explain that something/ someone was there with them and saved their life.

[33] Adapted from Cheryl Richardson's book, *Take Time for Your Life* (1999).

[34] For more help with this, see my book, *Freedom from Abuse: Finding Yourself Again* (2009).

[35] You may receive an audio of some of these meditation/visualization processes when you sign up for my mailing list at www.LoriRubenstein.com.

[36] Adapted from a process used by Dr. Richard Bartlett and Melissa Joy Jonsson at their Matrix Energetics Conference.

[37] Although I am not "certified" in EFT, I use it often in coaching and at retreats, with fabulous outcomes. There are a number of ways to do this, with various tapping points and various word algorithms. Feel free to employ whatever you are most comfortable using.

[38] Peter Rengel is a spiritual counselor living in California, whose poetry has touched my heart for many years. His other book, *Seeds of Light* is also filled with inspiration. He was truly awakened after a Near Death Experience in 1977 and chose to come back to tell us of the love he experienced.

[39] Because I wanted this book to have the utmost integrity, each person had to agree to use their own name in the stories. This is courage, and I thank them for it.

Self-Study and Book Club Study Aid

Self-study and Book Club Study Aid

What were you taught about forgiveness growing up?

As a child, what did the adults around you do regarding forgiveness, holding grudges, letting go, being judgmental, and talking negatively or positively about themselves and/or others?

Is there something in your life you have always considered "unforgivable?"

> Do you see that differently now? Can you describe the difference?

Is there something in your past that continues to haunt you? What will it take for you to let it go?

In chapter 2, we reviewed what forgiveness is and what it is not. Is there a forgiveness "myth" that you have held onto, such as 'to forgive means I have to condone the behavior?' Can you let it go; knowing now that it is not true?

As you were reading the book, did you have an ah-ha moment? What really clicked for you?

Do you believe the thoughts you think really create your future? If yes, what do you need to do/think/feel/believe to actually live like you believe this is true?

What is the hardest thing right now for you to let go of?

What is in the way of you letting go?

How would your life benefit if you did let go of it?

Go through the Living with Forgiveness Process (ARGG)

- Accept/Acknowledge
- Take personal Responsibility (at least for how you choose to respond)
- Find the Gift in the situation (what did you learn)
- Feel Gratitude for what you do have and who you are

What is the most difficult boundary you have had to set? How did you do it?

Is there a boundary you need to set with someone now? Who? Why? What is it?

Will you do it? What support do you need to do it?

What roles do guilt and shame play in your life? What does it do to you energetically? Can you commit to NOT beat yourself up for the past? What will it take for you to finally stop blaming yourself and to forgive YOU?

To maintain balance in your life, what MUST you do?

What is the most courageous thing you have ever done? How did it change your life?

If you are divorced, what is your real relationship with your ex? Are there any changes you can make? Did you do the higher self exercise? What were the gifts of your marriage and divorce? How can you honor your children's other parent even more, or do you need to set better boundaries? What does your inner-self tell you about this?

Forgiveness is about NOT blaming anyone else for who you are and how you feel about your life. Is there a piece of your life that you are not happy with?

> If yes, what do you need to change and what is the first step you need to take?

Who else do you need to forgive?

Do you continue to blame others? Can you see how it weakens you? Can you see that as long as you are blaming others, you give up your own power?

What would it look like for you to REALLY speak your truth?

How can you do your personal work, and God's work, with even more grace in your life?

Have you ever received a miracle after forgiving? What happened?

Can you describe your "old story" of anger, bitterness, resentment and hurt without the emotional drama-trauma?

What is your "new story?"

What is the next step on your path towards loving yourself even more?

Contributors

Contributors

I have been so blessed to know these authors and channels and I can tell you they are of the highest integrity. They have all agreed to use their real names in their stories so that YOU the reader understand that they too have had not only difficult journeys of their own, but that they are bravely standing firm out there in the world saying, this is my story!

From deep in my heart, I thank each one of you for your beautiful contribution towards make the book such a treasure and for seeing my dream, my vision, become a reality.

Forgiveness Stories

This book would not be made possible without the contributions of people who are courageously sharing their journey to forgiveness.[39] Each story is a gift, and I hope you receive the gift from these special contributors. We all need to remember that we all have stories, and our perception of those stories may be different than others. For some of the writers, it was like coming out of the closet, putting their life, their story, out there in the world to be judged by others – and that is scary. This is why I ask you to hold them in your hearts when you read their stories.

Channels

We truly are moving into the new golden age, and people who are gifted with the ability to communicate with those on the other side of the veil give us all the gift of being able to see things at a higher, more spiritual level. It gives us a perspective above and beyond what we would normally be able to receive.

In order of Introduction in the book

Contributor to Introduction:

Tarri Otterlee
Channeling Saint Germain

Tarri is a practicing Energy Therapist, medical intuitive for twelve years and does private readings for her clients. She is Healing Touch certified and a Traditional Usui Reiki Master/Teacher. Through her extensive training in these two healing modalities she feels they are the missing link to each other and now trains her students in both.

Years ago she incorporated Healing Touch into her holistic health care, and found it so successful for her own healing that she decided to go forward in her training to help others. Tarri has always had intuitive gifts, in the 1980's she was led to books and teachers that began her Spiritual journey. Through many years of growth and development and through her work as an Energy Therapist it led her to working with Spirit – The White Brotherhood "The Council of Light" helping and assisting her clients through deeper Spiritual healing sessions. Ten years ago Saint Germain from Spirit came to her requesting that she spiritually grow again to work with him and others from The White Christ Light to help and assist people in a greater way and to get his messages out in this time of great change of the earth which Spirit calls "The Shift of Awakening." As she has grown through Spirit/with Spirit she teaches and shares this with others who are on their journey.

Tarri spent twenty two years in health care, during this time she was a consultant and teacher to private practices. Her consulting and seminars took her throughout the United States, Canada, South Africa and England. She now calls herself semi retired living in Sedona, Arizona and doing the work she loves and calls her practice Perfect Balance.

Contributor to Chapter 3
Forgiveness: The Key to Spiritual Enlightenment

Dr. Earl Backman
Channeling the Light Beings

Earl Backman, Ph.D. is a former University Administrator and Corporate Executive. He is trained in mediation, conflict resolution, shamanism and soul regression. Earl is the administrator for The RavenHeart Center (www.ravenheartcenter.com); and works with his wife, Dr. Linda Backman, in coordinating the center's spiritual offerings, which include trainings, regression sessions, workshops, classes and lectures both in the US and abroad.

In addition, Earl is a Channel – receiving guidance from three beings from another celestial realm. He offers private channeling sessions, both in person and over the phone, as well as phone group channeling sessions once a month. Dr. Backman can be reached at
Earl@ravenheartcenter.com.

Contributors to Chapter 5

Our Greatest Teacher: Relationships – Finding Wholeness and Peace Through Lessons of Love and Letting Go

Debbie Dehm channeling Quan Yin

Debbie is a spiritual counselor, channel and tarot card reader and is available for session by telephone or in Hawaii, where she resides. She channels the Goddess of compassion, Quan Yin, who came to her ten years ago as a guide. She is also licensed in massage, reiki and reflexology.
For more information
www.compassionatehealing.biz
E-mail Debbie@compassionatehealing.biz

Susan Shammel

Susan Shammel lives in Ashland, Oregon and is a teacher, free-lance writer, and an advocate for disadvantaged youth. She has raised four teenagers and is currently developing an outreach program for women in divorce transition. She is passionate about personal growth and using adversity as a means for inner change and transformation.

Dr. Judy Chiger

Judy Chiger, MD, PhD, a holistic physician, is a teacher and guide helping professional women awaken to a healthy, balanced, energy-filled life. She leads them on a journey to discover their inner wisdom while befriending their inner critics. Dr. Judy can be contacted at www.drjudychiger.com or email@drjudychiger.com.

Michele Penn

Michele Penn lives in Sarasota, Florida, with David, the man of her dreams, where she finds great inspiration from a community rich in art-appreciation. In *Peace in the Present Moment*, Michele Penn's breathtaking floral photographs add peace and a deep stillness to the wisdom of Eckhart Tolle and Byron Katie. Michele's "soul shots" are a symbol of enlightenment. Her attention to detail and her ability to capture the soul of the flower sets her apart and makes her work truly inspiring. Michele is also one of 33 authors (including Lori Rubenstein) in *Faces Behind the Pages that Inspire*. Read about her journey of manifesting a book with two of the most spiritual authors of our era. Her three beautiful children, Freddy, Nicole and Melanie, fill her life with inspiration. As an award-winning photographer, inspiring speaker and business owner, she wants to enrich other people's lives.
www.CreativeElegancebyMichele.com
www.PeaceInThePresentMoment.net
www.facebook.com/peaceinthepresentmoment

Barry Costa

Barry Costa is raising his son who is now well adjusted. He has continued to pursue spiritual endeavors such as Shamanism, Matrix Energetics and other forms of healing.

Favorite quote . . . "When you change the way you look at things. The things you look at change." For more information go to www.BarryCosta.com

Terri Newlon
Channeling Djwhal Khul

Rev. Terri Newlon has channeled Djwhal Khul since 1980. She provides spiritual guidance online through teleseminars, private sessions, long-distance broadcasting, 12 Ray Attunements and free weekly spirituality articles. Terri has trained hundreds of people to channel their own higher self, ascended masters and angels. She shows other sensitives like herself how to turn on and off their psychic abilities in order to maintain a balanced life. The channeled teachings are practical, everyday spirituality that make living a better life easy. They are also very affordable. Terri lives in Patagonia, Arizona, USA with her partner Larry and their 3 beloved cats, ROQ, Rainbow and Sage. For more information: www.TerriNewlon.com

Contributors to Chapter 6
Forgiving the Unforgivable

Brenda Adelman

Brenda Adelman has a Master's degree in Spiritual Psychology, is an award-winning actor with a one-woman show about her life story and is the recipient of a Hero of Forgiveness award from the Hawaii International Forgiveness Project.

From the place of openness and strength she wrote a one-person show based on her life, titled *My Brooklyn Hamlet*, which she has performed internationally. She started teaching the steps she took to forgive to trainers in the domestic violence field, college students and youth at risk and has been blessed with the best relationship of her life. As her heart opened, so did her world. She speaks & leads teleseminars on The Heart & Art of Forgiveness and is a transformational life coach. Download her free e-course, The Five Top Reasons to Never Forgive and Why You Must at: www.forgivenessandfreedom.com

Immaculée Ilibagiza, Left to tell: Discovering God Amidst the Rwandan Holocaust (2007, Hay House, Inc., Carlsbad CA) story told with permission.

Christine Laureano
Channeling the Akashic Records
and telling her story

Christine Laureano (Ba6 Botanicals' Found & Chief Formulator, Entrepreneur, Life Coach and Co-author of the Amazon International Bestseller *Embracing Your Authentic Self*) LOVES to stand on a soapbox when it comes keeping it real and keeping it natural. Through her all natural, handcrafted skin care line, she shows women how to love the skin they're in because confidence is key in creating a Buff & Beautiful Life.

Christine has been there in her journey as small business owner, mentor/coach and entrepreneur. She found what made her stand out in the crowd of many and now helps other inspired women to create their lives, their businesses and their well being with intention and purpose. Christine's presentations are ideal for conference keynotes, breakout sessions, workshops and women's networking meetings.

Website: www.Ba6Botanicals.com
Email: Christine@Ba6Botanicals.com
Twitter: www.Twitter.com/CELaureano
Facebook:
http://www.facebook.com/Ba6Botanicals
Linkedin:
www.linkedin.com/in/christinelaureanocoaching

Sharon Lund, DD

Sharon Lund, DD is an inspirational speaker who has shared her life experiences and blessings to audiences throughout the United States, Canada, Europe, Russia and Japan. She has appeared on Oprah, 48 Hours, Eye on America, CNN, I Survived: Beyond and Back, and accepted an invitation from President Clinton to speak at the White House. Sharon was featured in the November 07 issue of "O" the Oprah Magazine. She is the author of the award-winning book *Sacred Living, Sacred Dying: A Guide to Embracing Life and Death,* as well as the author of *The Integrated Being: Techniques to Heal Your Mind-Body-Spirit, and There Is More . . . 18 Near-Death Experiences.* Sharon is the founder of Sacred Life Publishers and Sacred Life Productions. You may contact her through e-mail at Sharon@SacredLife.com and for more information www.SharonLund.com

Eva Kor's story from The Forgiveness Project used with permission from Ms. Kor.
www.candlesholocaustmuseum.org

Contributors to Chapter 7
Self Empowerment: Forgiving Ourselves and Forging Ahead Beyond Guilt and Shame

Mary Costanza

Some of her favorite quotes are, "Courage is looking fear right in the eye and saying, 'Get the hell out of my way, I've got things to do!'" ~ Craig Kurz

Maybe some women aren't meant to be tamed. Maybe they just need to run free til they find someone just as wild to run with them. ~ Unknown

Some of us aren't meant to belong. Some of us have to turn the world upside down and shake the hell out of it until we make our own place in it.

~ Elizabeth Lowell

http://www.facebook.com/marykcostanza
http://www.facebook.com/marycostanzaheartandsoul

Dr. Earl Backman
Channeling The Light Beings

Earl is a Channel – receiving guidance from three beings from another celestial realm. He offers private channeling sessions, both in person and over the phone, as well as phone group channeling sessions once a month. He can be reached at
Earl@ravenheartcenter.com

June Sedarbaum
Eugene, Oregon

Robby LeBlanc

Robby LeBlanc is an Author, Speaker, and Recording Artist. For More Information: www.RobbyLeBlanc.com

Charlene Stutes
Family Advocacy Consultant
charlenestutes@yahoo.com

Aazura
Channeling the Divine Union

Aazura is an author, teacher, healer and founder of the New Human Project™ dedicated to conscious transformation and awakening the heart. Aazura is recognized for the Acceleration Process™ for rapid freedom from 3D conditioning and belief structures of separation and limitation. She has been a messenger for ***Divine Union*** – Yeshua & Magdalene, teaching only love and healing our relationship with God, self and others. She is available for private sessions in person and via phone. Workshops & classes are offered. Aazura resides in Sedona, AZ. For more information:
www.NewHumanProject.com

Contributors to Chapter 8
Forgiving God

Shelly Collier
Cottonwood, AZ
shellyw@commspeed.net

Becca Tokarczyk, PT, M.Ed., IHT-MP
Beyond Grief, LLC
www.LifeBeyondSuicide.com

Acknowledgments

Acknowledgments

The goal of creating a book with a high level of integrity and spiritual consciousness does not happen alone. Each time I sat down, I felt guides and angels with me, guiding me to say what needed to be said. With deep gratitude and appreciation, I thank them.

My husband, Kevin, is my greatest supporter and the love of my life. I feel so loved, supported and taken care of, that the gratitude in my heart just spills over when I think about how fortunate I am to be so loved. On a more practical level, he gave me the space and time I needed to write, supported my self-imposed deadlines, and had to incessantly listen to me change my mind and process the title for this book. He gave me a great gift by helping me feel less embarrassed about my writing by reviewing drafts and correcting my grammar before I sent chapters off to my editor.

My editor, Lori Noble, is a forgiveness guru. I acknowledge and honor her spiritual practice which has brought her to a place where she herself is a forgiveness expert. Her support during the writing of this book was invaluable. It is my hope that I can encourage her to put her own writings out into the world for the public to appreciate. She is a great teacher in her own right and I am honored that she has agreed to work with me and support my vision for this project. She is like a sister to me.

I thank all the Channels: Aazura, Christine Laureano, Debbie Dehm, Earl Backman, Ph.D., Tarri Otterlee, and Terri Newlon, whose channelings have contributed to raising the vibration of this book in exactly the way I was hoping. They bring a beautiful gift to the world by allowing us to see and hear from the other side – our home.

The brave and courageous story tellers: Susan Shammel, Christine Laureano, Becca Tokarczyk, Charlene Stutes, Mary Costanza, Sharon Lund, Brenda Adelman, Barry Costa, Robby LeBlanc, Dr. Judy Chiger, Michele Penn, Shelly Collier, and June Sedarbaum. They gave the gift of being vulnerable, going public and opening their hearts so that you could learn from them, and understand how the gift of forgiveness can transform your life.

Christina Lufkin, author of "*Living with Purpose, Dying with Dignity*" for the name 'Living with Forgiveness' which has become my 4-step process, and for introducing me to Sharon Lund, who has become a dear friend and the publisher of this book.

Sharon Lund who has an incredible amount of patience, vision and wisdom, which she never withheld from me. Thank you for offering your publishing house, which is a beautiful force in the world, I am honored to be one of your selected authors.

On behalf of all the story and channel authors, we acknowledge YOUR courageous journey through pain into acceptance and forgiveness. We hold you big and it is with gratitude that all these stories are shared with you.

Lisa Love, whose ability to give life to a vision through her artistic talents, made this book cover a piece of art that truly makes me proud and speaks to the FEELING of the book.

Gail Alexander who designed a Mandela I used while writing this book for inspiration. It came with this message for the book: "Clearing the waves of forgiveness to help become whole, healed and live from a place of grace within your heart. It is about breathing in and moving through all the layers of forgiveness and reconnecting to your soul, spirit and divine spark."

My sister Staci for transcribing channeled messages.

Sunshower Rose for the adorable caricature of me with the dog, to help people remember the ARGG Living with Forgiveness Process.

Finally, I thank my parents, Larry and Karen, for being my champions from the other side of the veil, coming here to earth and being willing participants as young, naïve parents to a child with the potential to grow up and change people's view of divorce, abuse and forgiveness. I realize that if it were not for them, I would not have become the outspoken advocate I became. It's a great reminder of the paradoxes of this world, that sometimes our greatest supporters are the most unlikely ones.

About the Author

About the Author

Lori S. Rubenstein is a passionate lifetime learner in the art of forgiveness. She has been blessed with the gift of getting to practice forgiveness her whole life. She believes that our life path, our journey, is exactly what we need to meet our soul's desire, thus, there is a purpose and a reason for everything. Her life set her up perfectly to be a beacon – lighting the path for others to find their way back to love. Whether she holds you with grace and love, or a "tough-love-tell-it-like-it-is" attitude, you know this compassionate warrior has your back!

Lori's path included being raised by a teenaged mom in the projects and at age 4, her parents divorce. She visited with her father and step-mom weekly. Interestingly, after her mother remarried, they moved to a wealthy community so she was able to experience being both wealthy and impoverished. As a wild out of control teen, she spent time looking for love in all the wrong places, ending with a stint of one year in a drug rehabilitation center. She would not change one single event in her life, as it is the fabric of who she is and gives her the compassion to help others move through their own transitions.

After practicing law as a family attorney for 18 years, Lori is an example of someone who walks her talk. Twice divorced and having raised her two children, she is now in a new marriage to the man she has loved and adored for the last 6 years. Lori is honored to witness people's growth as she speaks to groups about forgiveness and moving through the transition from victim to victor!

Other books by Lori include:

- *Transcending Divorce: A Guide for Personal Growth and Transformation*
- *Conscious Relationships*
- *Freedom from Abuse: Finding Yourself Again*
- Co-authoring a best seller, *Wake-up Live the Life You Love*
- Co-authoring *The Faces Behind the Pages that Inspire*

To learn more about Lori, visit her Web site at www.LoriRubenstein.com for books, classes, retreats, meditations, visualizations, and workshop information.

CPSIA information can be obtained at www.ICGtesting.com
Printed in the USA
LVOW10s1310160115
423117LV00022B/391/P

9 780982 233160